Directory of Political Lobbying 2002

Justin Johnson

Politico's
PUBLISHING

First published in Great Britain 2002
by Politico's Publishing
8 Artillery Row
London
SW1P 1RZ
www.politicos.co.uk/publishing

A catalogue record of this book is available from the British Library

ISBN 1 84275 000 3

Printed by Bell & Bain Ltd., Glasgow

Contents

Introduction

The differences between this edition of Politico's *Directory of Political Lobbying* and its predecessor are immeasurable. People have changed, companies have come and gone, some merging, some splitting, and the industry as a whole has emerged unrecognisable from its former self.

The public affairs industry in the UK is one of the most advanced in Europe, yet one would have to look hard to find the 'archetypal' lobbying company. The companies listed in Chapter One vary in size from one employee to over a hundred. Political lobbying units can be found in law firms, public relations companies, management consultancies as well as being the main, but often not only, occupation of public affairs companies. In fact, the public affairs spectrum is far wider than this directory would imply. Virtually every sizeable organisation now has a dedicated public affairs unit, and sometimes they have monitoring teams as well. The spheres of public affairs consultancy and in-house teams are by no means separate, and a glance through Chapter Four, the Who's Who of UK Political Lobbying, will show that many players have worked in both worlds.

This directory focuses on companies that are primarily involved in political lobbying, or have a major consultancy arm devoted to lobbying. However, the term 'political lobbying' would be misleading. In fact, many of the companies in this directory actively avoid classifying themselves as such; 'we prefer not to think of ourselves as lobbyists' declares one company's mission statement. Looking through the company information for the listed UK companies in chapter one, it is possible to detect a more integrated approach to public affairs emerging from a number of companies. Public affairs units that are incorporated into public relations or law firms claim this to be an advantage. Access to a wide diversity of specialists and expertise, across disciplines, is claimed to provide a more 'comprehensive, yet customised' approach to political relations.

Whether this is the case has yet to be seen. The value of a more integrated service is likely to still depend on the demands of the project and the needs of the clients. There is still a definite space for individual lobbyists with unparalleled expertise and experience in their field, just as much as there is a need for companies to specialise in certain sectors or regions. What one can conclude is that because of its heterogeneity, the political lobbying industry now offers a previously unseen amount of choice and diversity. That public affairs has become such a broad and varied field hopefully guarantees the need for this directory, although it offers no promises about its 'shelf-life'.

In the public consciousness at least, political lobbying once implied 'privileged access', taking advantage of certain 'connections'. One colleague quipped that the shaking hands on the front cover should show a wad of cash changing hands. The associations with 'underhand' or undemocratic practices is perhaps part of the reason companies are eschewing the title 'political lobbying'. However it is a misleading caricature of the current scene. A quick scan through the company information in chapter one will pick out a number of common themes.

Never before has the ethical dimension been so prevalent in public affairs. For this reason, in chapter one, any 'Codes of Conduct' that companies might adhere to and any other statement of ethics or principles that the firm might use has been included. To supplement this, the Codes of Conduct for the APPC (the Association of Professional Political Consultants) and the PRCA (Public Relations Consultants Association) Public Affairs Committee can be found in chapter five. It is important to emphasise that the lack of any such code for a particular company in this directory simply means that none was obtainable, not that the company did not have one or adhere to one.

Beyond the renewed ethical dimension to public affairs, there is one of client empowerment. Throughout the company information in chapter one, one can see phrases such as 'believing the client is the best advocate'. The lobbying industry can no longer be seen as a gatekeeper to Westminster, versed in the skills of communication with those in positions of power. On the contrary, the lobbying industry works to demystify the labyrinthine processes in Brussels and the UK, to guide clients to where their voice can be heard most effectively. This surely is democracy in action. Those who comprise the NGO sector, the service sector, industry and business have no constituency, yet they must ensure their needs are considered in legislation and regulation.

The multifarious political lobbying industry has a key role in empowering the voices of clients, so politicians on all levels can respond to their needs. And the importance of this role can only grow. The raft of changes and developments in the way the United Kingdom runs itself means that increasingly there is no single route by which dialogue can be initiated with government decision-making. Power centres in Edinburgh and Cardiff as well as local and national government, mean lobbying companies have branched outside the traditional quarters of Westminster. To reflect this, where possible, all the relevant addresses for each company, not just the London ones, have been included. The increasing importance of the European Union (EU) in all spheres is reflected in chapter two, where EU lobbying companies are listed with their UK affiliates. This section can only to grow in future editions of this directory.

Finally, the advent of new technologies means that communication has been revolutionised. It's too soon to come to any conclusions about the impact of the communications revolution on public affairs. Concepts such as 'campaigning', 'accountability', 'pressure' and 'responsiveness' might all have to be redefined over the next few years. The advent of 'spin', and 24-hour news means political communication and the political agenda have changed beyond recognition. The thrilling challenge facing public affairs is how to respond. chapter six discusses this issue in some depth. Based on the DLA Upstream conference 'Lobbying in the 21st Century' held in late 2001, a number of views on the prospects for political lobbying in the technological age are aired. I am very grateful to Dr. Steve John of DLA Upstream for allowing us to publish the proceedings of their conference.

A brief mention must be made to the methodology used in formulating this directory. Virtually all the sources I have used are in the public domain. The information on the UK lobbying companies mostly comes from details given to me by the companies in question, and from their marketing literature. This directory does not intend to offer any value judgement for any particular company. Where no company information can be found in the directory, it is simply because no marketing literature was provided or obtained and bears no reflection on the firm in question. Some company information might seem more favourable to the company in question than others. If this is the case, it is simply an editorial error. I have explicitly attempted to be impartial when including company information, and reiterate that the intention of this directory is simply to provide a platform of information from which to find more about the lobbying industry.

The 'Who's Who' section in chapter three is by no means comprehensive – such an undertaking would require a separate directory of its own — it does however intend to give an overview of most of the key players in political consultancy and a brief biographical history of each one. Lastly, the merger of Weber Shandwick and GJW in late 2001 is part of the reason why the publishing date was put back a short while, and the full details of the new company, Weber Shandwick | GJW, can be found in Chapter One.

I am deeply grateful to the constant and fruitful advice given to be by Steve Atack, whose knowledge of the public affairs industry is unparalleled. However, the responsibility for any mistakes or inaccuracies in this directory is wholly my own. I would also like to thank Jim Boyd for his infectious enthusiasm about the idustry; John Berry at Politico's; and my ever-considerate friends, Jess, Sam and Nora, for putting up with me, and this directory. Finally, I would like to dedicate this book to the memory of my grandmother, Enid Haynes, who died earlier this year.

Justin Johnson
May 2002

1 UK Lobbying Directory

Advance Communications

Address	3/19 Holmbush Road
	London
	SW15 3LE
Telephone	020 8780 9110
Fax	020 8789 0795
E-mail	advance@portcullisresearch.com
Staff	7
Year of Formation	1992
Estimated Fee Income	£375,000
Associated Companies	Portcullis Research

APCO UK

Address	95 New Cavendish Street
	London
	W1M 7FR
Telephone	020 7526 3600
Fax	020 7526 3699
E-mail	mail@apco.co.uk
Edinburgh Address	APCO Edinburgh
	23a Blair Street
	Edinburgh
	EH1 1QR

| Telephone | 0131 225 6821 |
| Fax | 0131 220 4230 |

| Website | www.apcoworldwide.com |

Staff	45
Chairman	Simon Milton
Deputy Chairman	Rosemary Grogan
Managing Director	Nicholas DeLuca
Managing Director, APCO Scotland	Carol Aitken
Directors	Stephanie Ayres
	Simon Crine
	Martin Sawer
	Olly Grender

Year of Formation	1995
Parent Company	Grey Global Group
Associated Companies	GCI Political Counsel
Code of Conduct	APPC

Client List

ABB (UK) Ltd; Adflash; Advert Express Ltd; Alcatel; Audit Scotland; Aviation and Travel Consultancy; Britannia Airways; British Air Transport Association; British Battery Manufacturers; British Gas; British Generic Manufacturers Association; British Heart Foundation; British Railways Board; British Waterways; The Cancer Research Campaign; Carville (Scotland) Ltd; Castle Cement; Central Railways; Charles Schwab Europe; Chiltern Railway Company; Citigate Dewe Rogerson; Clear; CLH Ltd; College of Optometrists; Compass Roadside; Connex Transport (UK); DG Investments; Domestic & General; Dramay Holdings; East London Line Group; Energis; Enron Europe; Eurostar UK Ltd; Evening Standard; Fair Regulation Campaign; Financial Services Authority; Finex; First Group London Bus Operation; Foundation for Sport and the Arts; Fuel Cell System; Hamilton Clinical Waste; Hawksmere plc; Hospital Telephone Services; Interchange EMAP; International Trademark Association; The Internet Corporation; ITIS Holdings plc; Jarvis plc; JMC Airlines; Kent Reliance; Sir William Lithgow Bt; Littlewoods Leisure; Lloyds TSB Group; London Borough of Lewisham; London and Continental Railways; London Electricity; Marie Curie Cancer Care; Medical and Dental Defence Union of Scotland; Michael Hutchings Solicitors; Ministry of the Treasury (Poland); The Motorcycle Industry Association; National Association of Retired Police Officers; The Newspaper Society; Nomura (UK); OIS plc; Pace Micro Technology; PE International; Planned Savings Magazine; Prime Health; Procter & Gamble; Property Week; Punch Taverns; The Railway Forum; The Research Department; The Road Haulage Association; Rolls-Royce plc; Scientific Games International; Silverlink Train Services; Specsavers; Standard Life; Stannifer Developments; The Times; Toyota; Union Railways; Unisys; VGF plc; Woodland Trust; Zurich Municipals.

Company Information

Founded in 1995, APCO UK is now regarded as one of the country's leading consultancies. With offices in England, Scotland and Wales, the company has grown from a staff of six to a team of forty with backgrounds in government, politics, journalism, the civil service, business and think tanks.

After its first year, APCO UK was named the Best New Consultancy and two years ago won the PR Week award for Best Public Affairs Campaign 1999. APCO UK is also one of the first public affairs firms to be officially recognised as Investors in People.

The firm uses a variety of communications tools to help clients achieve their objectives, while being mindful of the importance of ethical conduct. Services range from traditional Westminster and Whitehall government relations programs to grassroots advocacy, coalition building, corporate community relations and media relations.

Their mission is to influence decision makers and shape public opinion by crafting compelling messages and recruiting effective political allies. They deploy their own and allied resources to build strong coalitions, organizing people at the grassroots and along the corridors of power. They support these efforts by employing ADAMS™, their grassroots mobilization software tool.

APCO monitors issues and develops and implements strategic lobbying campaigns that effectively influence policy makers. Armed with knowledge and in-depth experience with government institutions, they build support for a client's cause inside the halls of Congress, Parliaments, the EU, or any other governing entity. Similarly, they represent governments around the world by providing strategic counseling and public relations assistance.

AS Biss & Co

Address	100 Rochester Row
	London
	SW1P 1JP
Telephone	020 7828 3030
Fax	020 7828 5505
E-mail	tellmemore@asbiss.com/info@asbiss.com
Website	www.asbiss.com
Staff	25
Chairman	Adele Biss
Account Directors	Tim Payton
	Sacha Deshmukh
	Maureen O'Mara
Account Managers	Elliot Vaughn
	Lynette Huntley

	Sarah Atkinson
	Kate Ellis
Consultants	Sir Michael Partridge KCB
	Fred Silvester
	Roger Davies

Year of Formation	1996; incorporated Advocacy Ltd in 2000
Estimated Fee Income	£2.2m
Subsidiary Companies	Advocacy Ltd.
Brussels Office or Affiliate	Dedicated European Desk and officers managed from London and 'roaming' to Brussels
Trade Body Membership	APPC; PRCA; CBI

Code of Conduct

AS Biss company adheres to the APPC code of practice as well as having its own internal code and training on business ethics:

1   We undertake to uphold the "Seven Principles of Public Life" in all our dealings with those who serve the public in any way. These are set out on page 14 of the First Report of the Committee on Standards in Public Life chaired by Lord Nolan.
2   All members of staff have a confidential avenue through which they may raise any concerns about issues of probity. Anyone who is in doubt about the advisability or probity of any action or decision which could compromise or undermine adherence to the Seven Principles should immediately consult the managing director, chairman or nominated external consultant to the Company.
3   All staff have a duty of care to satisfy themselves that any representations which they make on behalf of clients, or those who are involved with public service, are honest and accurate.
4   No inducement may be given, offered or accepted in any of our business dealings which could reasonably be construed as in any way constituting a bribe or corrupt practice. Failure to observe this requirement may result in summary dismissal. We neither offer nor accept commission for the introduction of new business.
5   The Company will not pay any retainer or commission to any MP, MSP, AM, sitting Peer, MEP or person or company acting on their account; nor will the Company make any donation to a political party.
6   The Company is an equal opportunities employer. It expects its employees to be fair and unprejudiced in dealings and relationships with all people, without regard to race, religion, colour, gender, abilities, social background, sexual orientation or age.
7   This Code of Practice shall be on display in our offices. It will be appended to client contracts.

Client List

Adshel, Air Foyle, Association of Recognised English Language Services, Ashford's Future, Atlantic Estates Ltd, British Association for Shooting & Conservation, British Cargo Airline Alliance, British Shooting Sports Council, BT Payphones, Cadbury Schweppes plc, Cadbury Trebor Bassett Ltd, Camelot Group plc, Civil

Aviation Authority (Consumer Protection Group), Cityspace, Clydesdale Bank plc, ComCab plc, Commission for Racial Equality, Council for Registered Gas Installers, Domestic Violence Intervention Project, Dynegy UK Ltd, ELWa - Education and Learning Wales, Ewing Foundation, FA Premier League, F-Air Passenger Duty for all, Federation of Tour Operators, Fitness Industry Association, Foster Care Associates, Institution of Mechanical Engineers, ITV, ITV Digital, Joint Radio Taxi Association, The Library Association, London Taxi Board, Manganese Bronze Holdings plc, MEPC Ltd, More Group UK Ltd, Motor Industry Public Affairs Association, The Dairy Council, Nestle UK Ltd, Nuffield Hospitals, Parsons Brinckerhoff Ltd, PhoneSites Ltd, RAC Motoring Services, Resource - the Council for Museums, Archives and Libraries, Runnymede Lane, Sport England, Swiss Life (UK), TUI UK (Thomson Travel Group), Thames Passenger Services Federation, Winterthur Life (UK) Ltd, The Wastepack Group, Zurich Financial Services.

Company Information

AS Biss & Co now ranks in the top-ten of UK lobbying companies by turnover and is one of the largest independent players in the market. The company started by focussing on British regulatory, local and central government affairs but has now moved actively into European lobbying and devolved government work. London politics is a company speciality. AS Biss is now expanding from its public affairs base into wider corporate communications and reputation management.

Adele Biss has been active in communications for three decades, moving from marketing to advertising, the establishment of one of the UK's top PR companies and then as Chairman of the British Tourist Authority and English Tourist Board. She currently serves on the board of a number of organisations, largely in the travel and university education sector. Founding AS Biss in 1996 moved her directly into the public affairs arena, where she has now assembled a political team with a cross-party background, including active work in the trades union movement. Among the company's avowed aims is to bring business rigour to the public affairs industry.

AS Biss is a fast-growing corporate and public affairs independent consultancy. They are now one of the leaders in their field, operating across all the corporate communications disciplines. They cover a wide range of policy areas and sectors including financial services, travel and tourism, media and telecommunications, engineering, food and drink, property/planning and environmental services. Much of their recent expansion comes from the growing areas of the e-economy and corporate social responsibility.

Proud to be professional lobbyists, they believe that the shaping of legislation, regulation or public policy gains from the contribution of those most likely to be affected by it. Parliamentary and political relations, opinion forming and profile raising, in Westminster and Whitehall, Scotland and Wales and in the European Union form part of their everyday activity. They promise that their intellectual will can make sense of a complex brief, the communications skills to advance it successfully and the drive to make things happen.

August.One Public Affairs

Address	Network House
	Wood Lane
	London
	W12 7SL
Telephone	020 8434 5555
Fax	020 8434 5755
E-mail	publicaffairs.uk@augustone.co.uk
Address	August.One Public Affairs Scotland
	20 Forth Street
	Edinburgh
	EH1 3LH
Telephone	0131 550 3850
Fax	0131 550 3852
E-mail	publicaffairs.scotland@augustone.co.uk
Website	www.augustone.com/publicaffairs
Staff	11
Head of Public Affairs	Garry Walsh
Head of Influencer Relations	Rebecca George
European Client Specialist	Simon Thompson
Account Directors	Garry Walsh
	Lee Murgatroyd
Senior Policy Consultant	Susan Child
Senior Account Management	Theo Moore
Account Manager	Anthony Noun
Editorial Consultant	Gemma Burgess
Account Executives	PJ Bailey
	Chris Blundell
Parent Company	The Monday Group Plc (www.onemonday.com)
Associated Companies	Text 100 Global Public Relations
	(www.text100.com); Bite Communications
	(www.bitecomm.co.uk); Joe Public Relations
	(www.joepublicrelations.com); EVUS
	(www.evus.co.uk); Extra PR (www.extra-pr.de);

	Future Workplace Inc. (www.futureworkplace.com)
Brussels Office or Affiliate	Gellis Communications SPRL
Trade Body Membership	APPC; PRCA; a number of staff are also members of the IPR
Code of Conduct	APPC; PRCA

Client List

Microsoft (Scotland) Ltd, Microsoft EMEA, GartnerGroup, Gorbals Initiative, Citizens' Online, ETSU (AEA Technologies), Envirowise, Schoolmaster.net, SMG plc (Scottish Media Group), Virgin Radio, Integris (formerly Bull UK & Ireland), Content Technologies, Baltimore Technologies, Mencap.

Company Information

August.One Communications is a wholly owned subsidiary of the One Monday Group Plc. The group consists of a total of seven separate brands principally working within the technology PR market. August.One forms the second largest of these brands after Text 100, however, in the UK, August.One is the largest of the Group companies. While each brand has a separate business plan and management structure, it is not unknown for brands to co-operate on large, global accounts, giving August.One access to 23 offices in 16 countries worldwide.

Formed on 1 August 1999, August.One Communications is a spin-off from the global public relations company Text 100. It is a wholly owned subsidiary of the One Monday Group Plc (formerly Text 100 Group), which was founded in 1981 by Tom Lewis and Mark Adams on the same day that the IBM PC was launched. While retaining a strong bases in August.One's technology focused heritage, client wins such as SMG and Mencap have helped to lead the agency in new directions over the last year and this trend is set to continue.

Key successes, such as their involvement in the Electronic Communications Act, the Digital Britain Summit in June 2000, and co-ordinating talks between Michael Dell and Tony Blair, reaffirmed August.One's place as leaders in technology and public affairs.

Beaumark

Address	14 Great College St
	Westminster
	London
	SW1P 3RX
Telephone	020 7222 1371
Fax	020 7222 1440
E-mail	info@beaumark.ndirect.co.uk
Website	www.beaumark.co.uk
Year of Formation	1992

Trade Body Membership   APPC
Code of Conduct   APPC

Company Information

Beaumark is an independent political consultancy founded in 1992. The company is a member of the Association of Professional Political Consultants (APPC) and a signatory to the European Commission's and Parliament's public affairs codes.

The members of Beaumark's consulting team have direct experience of working in Government, Parliament, political parties, the European Parliament and the European Commission. With self-standing offices in Westminster and Brussels, the company can offer clients a detailed understanding and analysis of the British political system as well as European Union affairs. Many large organisations who undertake their own public affairs activities recognise the value of utilising external political auditors to provide an independent perspective of strategy and tactics.

Beaumark has considerable experience of undertaking such political and public policy audits. This work includes consideration of a client's internal policy and how it relates to the external political agenda. Externally, all public policy activities by Government, the UK and Scottish Parliaments, the Welsh assembly, political parties and EU institutions are analysed to identify their actual or potential impact on the client while internal communications structures are assessed against an agreed set of criteria. The resulting report has proved to be useful for clients when adapting their activities to the prevailing political climate.

The basis of any effective political relations campaign is detailed monitoring and analysis of the political process. Their monitoring service examines and analyses all relevant information distributed by the Government, the UK and Scottish Parliaments, the Welsh Assembly, political parties, think tanks and major pressure groups as well as the European Commission, Council of Ministers, European Parliament, Economic and Social Committee and the Committee of the Regions. The company also uses Parliament's 'Polis' and COI databases as well as the European Commission's and European Parliament's information databases.

Beaumark prides itself in its ability to accurately and quickly filter the vast amount of information distributed by these bodies. From an agreed base, they monitor developments on a daily basis, using a range of formal and informal techniques. By fully understanding the client's interests, it is possible to provide early warning of potential or actual issues which will impact upon the clients activities. The information is summarised and passed to the client with recommendations where appropriate. Staff are also available to cover Parliamentary Debates, Standing and Select Committee meeting and briefings in order to provide reports where official minutes or releases may not be available for some considerable time. Their location in the heart of Westminster enables them to cover such events with little notice.

Most large organisations usually undertake all representation themselves. In such situations Beaumark proposes a strategy for the client and offers advice on policy formulation, the key relevant opinion formers, and the approximate timetable for decisions to be taken on the issue. Clients are briefed on the most appropriate form of representation to make and how to adapt their case for the specific circumstances. Monitoring, as well as identification and profiling of relevant target audiences is also provided as a support service for the client.

Bell Pottinger Public Affairs

Address	16 Great College Street
	London
	SW1P 3RX
Telephone	020 7222 2096
Fax	020 7222 8550
E-mail	pbingle@bell-pottinger.co.uk
Address	Bell Pottinger Scotland
	1-3 Colme Street
	Edinburgh
	EH3 6AA
Telephone	0131 220 8294
Fax	0131 220 8394
Address	Bell Pottinger Wales
	Temple Court
	Catheral Road
	Cardiff
	CF11 9HA
Telephone	029 2078 6574
Fax	029 2078 6573
Website	www.bppa.co.uk
Managing Director	Paul Baverstock
Management Board	Kevin Murray
	David Beck
	Shimon Cohen
	Jon Tibbs
	Jerry Wood
	Tracey Spuyman
	Doug Richardson
	Patsy Baker
	Mark Seabright
Year of Formation	1988
Parent Company	Bell Pottinger Communications

Company Information

In the early nineties Bell Pottinger was known as the Lowe Howard Spink Group, subsequently becoming Lowe Bell. The former absorbed many familiar names in public relations including the respected Good Relations company. A further acquisition was the Russell Partnership, and the European Public Policy Group. The company is one of the giants of the Public Affairs Industry.

Bell Pottinger Public Affairs were the political advisers for CGNU in their £19 billion merger with Norwich Union. They also advised internet auction company QXL.com on a successful campaign to remove the National Insurance liability on share options granted to employees under unapproved corporate share option schemes. Channel 5, the UK's most recent terrestrial television channel appointed Bell Pottinger to advise on its public affairs issues.

Bircham Dyson Bell

Address	1 Dean Farrar Street
	Westminster
	London
	SW1H 0DY
Telephone	020 7222 8044
Fax	020 7360 1280
E-mail	jonathanbracken@bdb-law.co.uk
Website	www.bdb-law.co.uk
Staff	36
Year of Formation	1834
Brussels Office or Affiliate	Bircham Dyson Bell

Company Information

Bircham Dyson Bell is a Westminster based law firm which has been established in London for many years. In October 2000, Bircham & Co. combined its firm name with the name of its Parliamentary and Parliamentary Law department Dyson Bell Martin to become Bircham Dyson Bell.

Bircham Dyson Bell's Parliamentary and public law department specialises in all aspects of the law-making process, whether at a European, national or local level. This includes advice on influencing government policy and resulting legislation, advice on transport infrastructure and other major public works, public inquiries and promoting and opposing private and local legislation.

Services include:

*   Drafting of all forms of primary and secondary legislation and advice on Parliamentary and Assembly procedures (European Parliament, U.K. Parliament, Scottish Parliament, National Assembly for Wales and Northern Ireland Assembly).

- Promotion of and opposition to private bills in the U.K. and Scottish Parliament and the Northern Ireland Assembly.
- Promotion of and opposition to local transport, compulsory purchase and infrastructure schemes.
- Advice on the constitution and regulation of ports, harbours and conservancies.
- A wide range of planning and environmental work, often involving lengthy public inquiries.
- A wide range of advice on public law issues such as human rights, public procurement, judicial review and statutory challenge.
- Monitoring legislative and policy developments at the European and U.K. levels and within the devolved administrations and advice on influencing the processes concerned

BKSH

Address	24–28 Bloomsbury Way
	London
	WC1A 2PX
Telephone	020 7300 6160
Fax	020 7404 2360
Website	www.bksh.com
Director	Alan Butler
Manager	Frances Luff
Associates	Stuart Bugg
	Anna Lucuk
	David Robinson
Parent Company	UK Government Affairs arm of Burson-Marsteller

Client List

Accenture; Baccardi Martini; BD; Cumbria Tourist Board; Exide Technologies; Cray Valley; Government of Kuwait; HongKong Jockey Club; International Euroasian Democracy Foundation; Iraqi National Congress; Magistrates' Association; National Air Traffic Services; Pharmaceutical Schizophrenia Association; Strathclyde Passenger Association; Tate and Lyle; Telewest; Tesco; Transworld.

Company Information

The BKSH company literature poetically explains that "The raft of changes and developments in the way the United Kingdom runs itself means that increasingly there is no single route by which influence can now be brought to bear on government decision-making. It is now necessary for clients to regard the political landscape as if it were an orchestra, with different sections influenced in stages until all can be persuaded to play the same tune."

Fundamental to BKSH's strategy is the that clients recognise that they are their best advocate. The role of BKSH is to draw on its experience to advise the client on strategy and tactics while using its own network within the government, Parliament, civil service, media and political parties. They offer a seamless pan-European government relations service with parts of a 100-strong public affairs practice in Europe.

Burson-Marsteller

Address	24-28 Bloomsbury Way
	London
	WC1A 2PX
Telephone	020 7300 6468
Fax	020 7300 6145
E-mail	vickie_morgan@uk.bm.com
Website	www.bm.com
Staff	186
Chair and MD, Public Affairs, Burson-Marsteller, Europe	Gavin Grant
CEO and President Burson-Marsteller, UK	Allan Biggar
Managing Director	Jeremy Galbraith
Manager Head	Frances Luff
Chairman, BKSH Europe	Peter Linton
Vice-Chairman, BKSH Europe	John Robinson
Directors, BKSH	Robert Mack
	Elizabeth De Bony
	John Duhig
Public Affairs Associates	David Robinson (BKSH)
	Stuart Bugg (BKSH)
	Anna Lucuk (Burson-Marsteller UK)
Research and Monitoring Staff	Elaine Ward
	Emmanuella Tsapouli
Year of Formation	Founded by Harold Burson and Bill Marsteller in 1953; subsidiary of Young & Rubicam Group since 1977; part of WPP Group since September 2000

Estimated Fee Income	£17m
Parent Company	Young & Rubicam; ultimate holding company is WPP
Subsidiary Companies	Communique Public Relations Ltd; Government Affairs arm is BKSH
Associated Companies	i-syt, joint venture with BM UK, established April 2000
Brussels Office or Affiliate	Burson-Marsteller Brussels (BKSH)
Trade Body Membership	PRCA

Client List

It is not the policy of Burson-Marsteller to give out confidential client information, however the names in the public domain include: 3I, 3COM, Accenture, Agriflow, Alcatel, Association of Tennis Players, Astra Zeneca, Bird's Eye Walls, BP Amoco, British Telecommunications plc., Citibank, Danone, DEGW, Digital Mobility, eBookers, Eli Lilly, Fox Kids Europe, GlaxoSmithKline, Jim Beam Brands, Johnson & Johnson, L'Oreal, Merck Sharp & Dohme, Multex Investor Europe, Philip Morris, Prudential, Qualcomm, Roche, Sanofi, SABIC, Sodexho, Transora, Unilever, Visteon, Xworxs.

Company Information

The European flagship office for Burson-Marsteller, one of the world's largest communications consultancies, B-M London is a dynamic and creative PR agency dedicated to delivering insightful strategy and ideas for boards and their brands.

Clients are UK specific and multinational, covering a broad range of companies – from large public to private firms, as well as professional, government and non profit organisations. Shamelessly building 'unfair advantages' for clients, Burson-Marsteller increasingly provides integrated communications.

Specific expertise includes media relations, financial and corporate communications, public affairs, crisis communications, change communications, issues management, brand marketing, technology, healthcare, corporate social responsibility, new media & e-commerce and executive coaching/media training. In addition, B-M London is home to a branch of premiere public affairs agency BKSH, (BKSH is the Government Affairs arm of Burson Marsteller) as well as Marsteller, the world-renowned advertising agency and i-syt, the technology convergence joint venture created last year to ensure B-M can deliver clients' visions.

In May 2001 B-M London acquired Communique PR, the highly respected Manchester-based consultancy to become B-M UK.

Butler Kelly

Address	28 Eccleston Square
	London
	SW1V 1NS
Telephone	020 7932 2410
Fax	020 7932 2411
E-mail	admin@butlerkellyltd.co.uk
Website	www.butlerkellyltd.co.uk
Staff	7
Directors	Chris Butler
	Phil Kelly
Senior Consultant	Phil Royal
Consultants	David Nicholson
	Terry Ashton
	Hugo Summerson
Researcher	Kate Archer
Year of Formation	1998
Estimated Fee Income	under £1m
Trade Body Membership	APPC; some staff are members of the NUJ and the TGWU
Code of Conduct	APPC. Butler Kelly have also called for Parliamentary regulation and oversight of the lobbying industry. They do not pay or have financial relationships with MPs, Peers, or other public representatives. Internally, they operate a conscientious objection policy – they would not work to promote tobacco or for dubious foreign governments, for instance.

Client List

Allied Deals plc, Angel Trains, British Aerospace (BAE Systems), British Secondary Metals Association, BT Syntegra, Cable Companies Association, Calor Gas, Capital Radio, Cegelec-CGA, Commercial Radio Companies Association, Edex, Eli Lilly and Company, Engelhard, Enron Europe, Environment Agency, FRES, General Healthcare Group, Iceland Frozen Foods plc, JCDecaux UK, Kingston Communications plc, Logica, London International Group, Mainline Freight, Medihealth, M40 Trains, Newlon Housing Association, Nomura International, NPI, Pearson Television, Radio Advertising Bureau, Railtrack, Reliance Europe, Redstone

Telecom, Rotch Properties, S4C, Swedish Match, Telewest Communications plc, The D Group, United Kingdom Accreditation Service, West Ham United plc, Wilton Park Conference Centre.

Company Information

Butler Kelly Ltd. an independent cross-Party public affairs consultancy established in 1998. The two founder Directors are Phil Kelly and Chris Butler, who started their business association with the formation in 1995 of a public affairs unit in one of the UK's leading public relations consultancies. They:

- Offer a full political monitoring service, covering Government and parliamentary publications, statements, documents and speeches relevant to corporate interest.
- Liase between business, Whitehall, Westminster and local authorities, when making cases to the Government or the Opposition's policy-making machine.
- Indicate which politicians and officials relevant to particular cases, and how to communicate with them.
- Negotiate settlements acceptable to officials when handling Bills, averting adverse legislative change and effecting beneficial amendments as bills to go through.
- Considerable programme of Select Committee Preparation. Former MPs with Select Committee experience provide training with video recordings, briefings on procedure, full profiles of the Committee members and advice on dealing with the Clerk to the Committee.
- Advice on Local Government, including public private partnerships, planning and regeneration, to minimise opposition. Helped local authorities make their case to central Government.
- Executive communication instruction and event organisation

CDC Public Affairs

Address	7 Marsham Street
	Westminster
	London
	SW1P 3DW
Telephone	020 7222 2772
Fax	020 7222 2773
Website	www.cdcpublicaffairs.com
Year of Formation	1987
Subsidiary Companies	CDC Public Policy Monitoring

Company Information

CDC Public Affairs operate from the heart of Westminster. They offer a specialist public affairs service where they help their clients every step of the way. Whether dealing with Ministers, commissioners, protesters, councillors or local residents, CDC's broad based staff cover the spectrum and are able to help. Cliff Davis-Coleman founded the company in 1987 with a background in journalism and a degree in public administration. He believed that the existing lobbying companies were too academic in their approach and what was required was a more shirt-sleeved approach to guiding and assisting companies through the legislative maze.

CDC Public Policy Monitoring is a new tailor-made service designed to enable clients to get the most out of Westminster and Europe. The service is entirely e-mail based and provides the relevant details of parliamentary business for clients' areas.

Central Lobby Consultants

Address	12 Little College Street
	Westminster
	London
	SW1P 3SH
Telephone	020 7222 1265
Fax	020 7222 1250
E-mail	info@central-lobby.co.uk
Staff	7
Managing Director	Helen Donoghue
European Account Director	Heather Cantley
Head of Research and Information	Helen Nicholson
UK Account Director	Mark McLaren
Account Executives	Damien Hall
	Katherine Angel
Information Technology	Mike Hale
Year of Formation	1984
Trade Body Membership	IPR Government Affairs Group

Client List

CLC's current client list is drawn from public companies, European networks, trade associations, enterprise bodies, individual charities, charitable and cross-sector umbrella bodies and Parliamentary Groups. They specialise in energy and environmental issues; taxation; voluntary sectors issues; food and health; long-term care and funding; social and educational policy; and rural and urban policy.

Company Information

Central Lobby Consultants Ltd is a well-established, independent consultancy, which has specialised in government affairs and political analysis in the UK and within the EU since 1984.

At CLC, they offer clients a comprehensive public affairs support service tailored to client objectives and resource priorities. In practice, that means that they first assess objectively whether a prospective client needs a public affairs service. They have build up long term, close working relationships with their clients, and they will also undertake specific short-term projects. Their services are based on their broad information and intelligence sources, their sound knowledge of the UK and the EU legislative and political processes and their keen political judgement.

How they deliver their services has been changing, for instance they now provide online information by means of tailored client websites. Yet, however much technology and methods of service delivery may change, their services are provided within an enduring ethos of assessing the merits and validity of a case; recognising the proper limits within which lobbying activity can and should be conducted; and respecting the integrity of clients and policymakers.

Chelgate

Address	Number One Tanner Street
	London
	SE1 3LE
Telephone	020 7939 7939
Fax	020 7939 3938
E-mail	admin@chelgate.com
Website	www.chelgate.com
Staff	30
Chairman and Chief Executive	Terence Fane-Saunders
Finance Director and Company Secretary	Mathew Lane
Executive Vice-Presidents	Nicholas Wood-Dow
	Frank Wingate
	Tony Brown
	James Darley
	Bene't Steinberg
	Leo Cavendish
	Mark Pinkstone
Senior Counsellors	Mary Derrane
	Mark Glover
	John Grimley
	Michael Hardware

Penny Mack

Mark Pursey

Michael Wilson

Andrew Moore

Year of Formation	1988
Estimated Fee Income	over £2m
Subsidiary Companies	RBC International (graphic design and advertising);
Associated Companies	network of associates and affiliates
Trade Body Membership	Some staff are members of MIPR; Institute of
	Management; Chartered Institute of Management

Company Information

Chelgate is an independent, international PR firm, headquartered in London with branch offices in Asia and a network of associates across continental Europe and around the world. Chelgate's own style is unusually discreet and low-profile, but its clients include some of the UK's best-know businesses and a broad spread of major multinationals.

Chelgate eschew the title of 'lobbyist', associating it with 'guns for hire'. They tend to think that their clients are the best advocates for their own cause, and Chelgate's job is to create the opportunity, identify the appropriate channels and help the client shape the best possible case. It is not expected that friends in Parliament should extend special rights or privileges. However, when an MP, minister or special adviser knows they can expect an accurate, well-informed case, without trickery or deception, they will be inclined to respond positively. The same rule applies to dealing with the press. With this in mind Chelgate has no compunction about asking an MP to ask a Parliamentary Question. This is seen more as democracy in action, as MPs are there to listen and represent. As well as boasting a first class Government Relations business, Chelgate believes it is vital to have a good understanding of what Government in planning. This means effective and professional monitoring and feedback.

In its local government work, Chelgate has two separate offerings. It works both on behalf of companies wishing to talk with local government and on behalf of councils in managing their relationships with their many stakeholders, including the local communities which they serve. Chelgate is able to do this because both roles require the same skills base: knowledge of politics and local government, of local communities and the media they read and of business. They monitor current development and maintain an updated understanding of local government and local communities and how they are evolving under new structures. Their team offers extensive experience of the government associations, and includes both current and former councillors.

Cherton Enterprise

Address	Tweskard Mews
	313 Belmont Road
	Belfast
	BT4 2NE
Telephone	028 9076 3399
Fax	028 9076 9377
E-mail	staff@cherton.co.uk
Website	www.cherton.co.uk
Staff	5
Chairman	William T Pinkerton
Managing Director	Robin C Guthrie
Finance Director	Muriel M McCutcheon
Account Director	Siobhan Donnan
Account Executive	Sally Buckley
Year of Formation	1995
Estimated Fee Income	£300,000
Parent Company	Cherton Enterprise Limited
Trade Body Membership	APPC; PRCA (Assoc.)
Code of Conduct	APPC

Client List

Sainsbury's Supermarkets Ltd, Stannifer Developments, Land Securities, Morrison Development Partnerships Ltd, Aquis Estates & Anglia & General, Phoenix Natural Gas, Andras House, Westfield Shopping Centre, B&Q, H3g, Farrans, McCormick Properties Ltd.

Company Information

Cherton Enterprise Limited was founded in 1995 when its two founding partners identified a niche opportunity in the Northern Ireland marketplace for a professional PR/public affairs company specialising in, but not exclusive to, the property development market. The experience of the principals in the public sector but dealing almost entirely with major private commercial projects enabled them to identify the areas where companies, especially, but not exclusively, those new to the Northern Ireland scene, required specific professional advice.

Through its well developed networks with local business media and all levels of the Public Sector, Cherton will: promote the virtues of clients and proposals; identify problems and probably opposition to proposed projects or developments; develop strategies to develop and counter these; co-ordinate and implement agreed strategies in partnership with the client and other professional advisers. Specific services include: access to Government and the administration; access to all political parties; lobbying/PR programmes; media management, including briefings, press releases; access to business institutions; preparation of brochures/marketing material; public exhibitions; community lobbying.

Cicero

Address	56-60 Gresham Street
	London
	EC2V 7BB
	Due for relocation, Jan 2002
Telephone	020 7776 6555
Fax	020 7726 6544
E-mail	info@cicero-europe.com
Website	www.cicero-europe.com
Staff	10
Non-Executive Chairman	Jon Schwartz
Chief Executive	Stephen Lock
Chief Operating Officer and Finance Director	Sunil Sharma
Executive Director and Chief Corporate Counsel	Iain Anderson
Executive Director and Chief Political Counsel	Richard Elsen
Non-Executive Director	Jeremy Swan
Account Director	Melanie Riley
Account Executive	Peter Shackleton
Associate	Amanda Atkinson
Year of Formation	2001, founded by the Ludgate Public Affairs management team
Brussels Office or Affiliate	Planned launch of Brussels office, September 2001
Trade Body Membership	APPC; all fee-earning staff are required to be members of the IPR

Code of Conduct

APPC, which all staff members must individually read and sign every six months. In addition to which:

- All UK fee-earners are required to be members, or to apply for membership to the IPR;
- Cicero encourages its employees to participate in the democratic process, but all such activity must be disclosed to the Chief Executive;

- Employees elected to Parliamentary (or equivalent) body of the country in which they are employed are required immediately to submit their resignation;
- Cicero will generally not accept work from any Government or Head of State not democratically elected, except in circumstances where such representation is directly connected to the managed transition to democracy;
- Cicero will not work for corporations or individuals primarily engaged in arms manufacture or trading;
- Cicero fully complies with the Political Parties, Elections & Referendums Act 2000 and has appointed its Company Secretary to act as Compliance Officer of its provisions;
- In its Litigation PR practice, Cicero will not represent any corporate or individual defendant in any criminal trial before a jury, but reserves the right – at its discretion – to represent corporate or individual defendants in criminal trials (not being before a jury);
- Cicero will obey the Contempt of Court rules of every jurisdiction in which it operates
- Cicero will not represent any individual or entity (corporate or otherwise) charged with crimes against humanity and will generally not work with any individual or entity on any other mandate even where not connected to such charges;
- All Cicero suppliers are required to sign confidentiality agreements with the Consultancy and are specifically required to state their adherence to, and liability for, all criminal and civil laws in the jurisdictions in which they operate.

Client List

Clients January to 31 July 2001. Cicero also has a 'private client' practice, in addition to the corporate names listed: Aberdeen Asset Management Plc; Aberdeen Unit Trust Managers Ltd; Alliance & Leicester plc; Elite Model Management SA; Eurasian Bank of Kazakhstan; Inaura (pro bono client – education charity); Kazakhstan Metallurgical Group (BVI); Kika Investments; National Consumer Council; Nike UK; Retirement Income Reform Campaign; Sanyo Europe; Tommy Hilfiger Europe; Unum Limited; Viasystems Group Ltd.

Company Information

Cicero Consulting, named by PR Week in its 2001 'Top 150' survey as the public affairs 'One to Watch' offers its clients public affairs and government relations, including legislative lobbying, corporate reputation management, including crisis communications, litigation PR and strategic advice on Internet-based public corporate campaigns and fast, sophisticated Internet monitoring and intelligence services. Their goal is to be outstanding for their clients, trusted by them to exceed their expectations. In doing so they aim to be admired, rather than popular, respected, rather than famous, the best, rather than the biggest.

Cicero Consulting Limited is the 'public interest' issues management consultancy for Europe that specialises in Litigation PR; Government relations and political affairs; corporate crisis PR management and 'public campaigning'. The firm is named after the Roman figure of Marcus Tullius Cicero (106-43 BC) who has for centuries been recognised as the 'father of rhetoric'. Cicero is an independent, privately owned company whose shareholders include its directors and staff.

Cicero is headquartered in London and in Autumn 2001 shall open offices in Paris and Brussels. Their Paris office will offer clients Litigation PR; French government relations and public affairs and will offer a particular expertise in PR management. Their Brussels office will be able to assist clients in all the diverse aspects of lobbying 'Brussels DC', as well as offer clients a specialist PR service directed towards the press corps covering the European Parliament and other EU institutions. In addition to these offices, Cicero has carefully selected affilitate consultancies in a number of other European territories, including Austria, Germany, Italy, Poland, Russia, Spain and Turkey. Cicero also has connections with firms outside Europe, if required.

Cicero offers clients specialist public affairs and PR services. The Cicero founders have advised clients operating in a number of different sectors, particularly Government and public sector; chemicals; financial services; retailing; telecoms and technology; mining, oil and gas; transport and environmental services.

Citigate Public Affairs

London Address	26 Grosvenor Gardens
	Westminster
	London
	SW1W 0GT
Telephone	020 7838 4800
Fax	020 7838 4801
Cardiff Address	The Executive Centre
	Temple Court
	Cathedral Road
	Cardiff CF1 9HA
	Wales
Telephone	029 2078 6434
Fax	029 2078 6435
Edinburgh Address	Conference House
	152 Morrison Street
	The Exchange
	Edinburgh EH3 8EB
	Scotland
Telephone	0131 200 6040
Fax	0131 200 6144
E-mail	info@citigate.co.uk
Website	www.citigatepa.co.uk
Staff	48
Executive Director	Simon Nayyar
Managing Director	Warwick Smith

Head of CPA Wales	Marc Evans
Head of Political Intelligence Unit	Suzanne Fenteman
Head of Brussels Office	Thierry LeBeaux
Head of Scotland Office	John Mullin
Directors	David Bennett
	Louise de Winter
	Rex Osborn
	Jonathan Roberts
	Account Directors
	Joanne Bullen
	Paul Duke
	Richard Gibson
	James Nason
Consultants	Charles Miller
	Steven Norris
	Carole Tongue
Year of Formation	1968
Estimated Fee Income	£3.5m
Parent Company	Incepta Group plc
Associated Companies	Beaumark
Brussels Office or Affiliate	Citigate Public Affairs
Code of Conduct	PRCA

Company Information

Areas of expertise: Government communications, issues management, event management, crisis public relations, environmental issues.

Clarion Communications

Address	121–141 Westbourne Terrace
	London
	W2 6JR
Telephone	020 7299 9100
E-mail	enquiries@clarioncomms.co.uk
Website	www.clarioncomms.co.uk

Year of Formation   1986
Parent Company   Part of the Cordiant Communications Group

CMA Group

Address   27 Albemarle Street
                                           London
                                           W1X 3FA
Telephone   020 7495 5040
E-mail   malmac@dial.pipex.com
Website   www.malmac.dial.pipex.com

Company Information and Notes

Malcolm McIntyre represents the CMA group, and uses his career as a writer, editor and public affairs consultant to discretely lobby on behalf of clients. He claims inside knowledge of Parliamentary procedure and contacts at all levels of Government and the Civil Service, as well as in the three main UK political parties. Among his successes, he led the defence of the UK's 3,500 motor traders when the faced an enquiry into a possible commercial monopoly and won a further eight years of profitable non-interference. He was awarded a Chavalier of one of France's oldest commercial orders after he restored the French Champagne industry's fortunes in the UK. He is an independent, old school political lobbyist with considerable success under his belt.

Commonwealth Consultants Bureau

Address   22 Hazlewell Road
                                           London
                                           SW15 6LH
Telephone   020 8789 6632
Fax   020 8392 1410
E-mail   rjdm@genie.co.uk

Proprietor   Richard Moir
Consultants   Maria Dixon
                                           Ian MacFadyen
                                           Dr Arthur Owen
                                           Damian Perl

Nicholas Roche

Peter Voss

Robert Knowles

Year of Formation	1999
Trade Body Membership	Richard Moir is a member of the IPR and the Foreign Press Association

Client List

Various Embassies, Commonwealth High Commissions and private companies.

Company Information

Commonwealth Consultants Bureau is a unique multi-disciplinary team designed to promote Commonwealth member countries in the new millennium, particularly those of Afro-Carribean and Asian origin, in their relations with the UK (Regional Assemblies, Westminster and Whitehall), the World Trade Organisation, European Union, and on a country-by-county basis, through lobby, trade promotion, representation and issues management. They teach their clients to market themselves to existing and evolving political infrastructures so as to promote inward/outward investment; access to grants and so on. They offer a fully integrated range of services from political and media counsel; regulatory advice; scientific/technical services; security and crisis management; to the organisation of seminars and promotions at trade fairs, for those wanting to develop relationships with the UK Government, the European Union and beyond. They believe it is crucial that the Commonwealth be given better representation as the UK moves closer to Europe so that the Commonwealth can be explained in modern terms. It is even more important for them to establish links with Europe and European national parliaments.

The Communication Group

Address	19 Buckingham Gate
	London
	SW1E 6LB
Telephone	020 7630 1411
Fax	020 7931 7800
E-mail	political@thecommunicationgroup.co.uk
Website	www.thecommunicationgroup.co.uk
Brussels Office or Affiliate	Entente International Communication SA

Company Information

As the UK and European political scene evolves, more and more organisations recognise the need to communicate with government and political decision-makers. The Communication Group boasts an outstanding track record on major political issues, advising clients on strategy and helping them present compelling cases.

Whether a client wants to brief key opinion formers or reach out via journalistic briefing programmes, the political division of The Communication Group offers its help. Claiming that the key to success is the ability to monitor political action, they boast that their expertise in research and intelligence will keep their clients ahead of the game. Furthermore, their powerful resource in Brussels means they can link up with European political agendas too.

Connect Public Affairs

Address	Millbank Tower
	Millbank
	London
	SW1P 4QP
Telephone	020 7222 3533
Fax	020 7222 2677
E-mail	info@connectpa.co.uk
Website	www.connectpa.co.uk
Staff	15
Chairman	Andrew Gairdner
Managing Director	Gill Morris
Deputy Managing Director	Malcolm George
Directors	Steve Barwick
	Mike Mason
Account Directors	Emily Wallace
Account Manager	Gazala Haq
Consultant	Simon Redfern
Conference Producers	Fiona Ross
	Kenny Mizzi
Research Consultant and Head of Monitoring	Michael Burns
Research Consultant	Richard Wiltshire
Research Executive	Kate Coleman
Year of Formation	1998
Estimated Fee Income	£1.5m
Brussels Office or Affiliate	'By virtue of our independence we work with a range of European associates and partners

that best suit client requirements'.

Trade Body Membership   APPC; PRCA; IPR Government Affairs Group

Code of Conduct

Founding member of the APPC and fully subscribes to their code. Connect places great emphasis on probity and believes that the client is the best advocate. Connect was the first public affairs company to be awarded Investor in People accreditation.

Client List

Abbey National, Advertising Association, Agents Association, Astra Marketing, British Agencies for Adoption and Fostering, British Telecom and Post Office Pensioners, Chartered Insurance Institute, Crisis, Elmbirch, Ford Motor Company, Greater Manchester Passenger Transport Executive, Ineos Fluor, Iron and Steel Trades Confederation, JCDecaux, Language Line, National Association of Estate Agents, National Right to Fuel Campaign, New Opportunities Fund, Nirex, Oasis Healthcare, Places for People, Plurge (Public Utility Reform Group), Rail Passengers Council, Regional Policy Forum, Rehab UK, Royal Pharmaceutical Society of Great Britain, Society of Chiropodists and Podiatrists, South African Breweries, Tesco Stores, Thames Gateway London Partnership, Unifi, Unison, WWAV Rapp Collins, Zurich Financial Services.

Company Information

Connect Public Affairs was originally formed in 1990 by Mike Craven, as a subsidiary to Market Access, to specialise in public affairs consultancy in the non-commercial and trade union sector. In 1994 Market Access (and therefore Connect) was bought by Omnicom. In February 1996 Connect Public Affairs merged with Government Policy Consultants (GPC), also owned by Omnicom, to form a single company GPC Connect, and Gill Morris became Managing Director of the new company.

In 1997 the Canadian owned GPC, became wholly owned by Omnicom and it was subsequently agreed that the GPC branding should transfer to the bigger UK brand Market Access to form a single public affairs brand in Europe. This decision would have meant that both Market Access and GPC Connect; their clients and staff would merge into a single European-wide company to form GPC. This was deemed to be unacceptable by GPC Connect and a new proposal was promoted by GPC Connect to effectively buy the company from Omnicom. A management buy-out led to the formation of Connect Public Affairs Ltd – as an independently owned company – on 1 January 1998. Connect's new found independence and past reputation provided a good platform to grow. Connect launched Connect Corporate in 2001. Connect Corporate provides strategic counsel to corporate clients and sits alongside their other brand services, Connect Conferences and Connect Politics.

By developing new and distinct products and services Connect have been able to build on their past recognition and establish a broader client base.

Connect Politics monitoring and research staff have backgrounds in Parliament, local government, charities and private sector companies. The political e.monitoring service provided by Connect Politics provides the client with a secure, easy to navigate, pass-coded client web monitoring account which is updated daily with relevant extracts from all available sources.

Consolidated Communications Public Affairs

Address	1-5 Poland Street
	London
	W1F 8PR
Telephone	020 7287 2087
Fax	020 7734 0772
E-mail	publicaffairs@consol.co.uk
Website	www.consol.co.uk
Staff	8
Managing Director (of CCPA)	Edward Vaizey
Chief Executive (of CCM Ltd)	Sarah Robinson
Director	James Boyd
Account Directors	Ilan Jacobs
	Richard Jarman
Senior Account Executives	Sarah Cotton
	Angela Pollock
Account Assistants	Dominic Masterton-Smith
	Beth Druce
Year of Formation	1998
Estimated Fee Income	£600,000
Parent Company	Consolidated Communications Management
Trade Body Membership	APPC; PRCA; some staff are members of the MSF
Code of Conduct	APPC

Client List

Alcatel, AskJeeves, Britannic Retirement Solutions, British Venture Capital Association, Commission for Racial Equality, Co-operative Insurance Society, Countryside Alliance's Campaign for Shooting, Eastern Regions Pharmaceutical Group, Go-Ahead Group, Institute & Faculty of Actuaries, Napp Pharmaceuticals, Ninja Corporation, Rank Group – Mecca Leisure, Scottish Provident UK, Stonewall, thetrainline.com, Victor Chandler International, Virgin Direct, virginmoney.com, Virgin Mobile, Walt Disney Corporation, World Vision, Zurich Financial Services.

Company Information

The Company was founded by former lawyers Edward Vaizey, Managing Director and Jim Boyd, Director in 1998. Since its start the company has been credited with being one of the most successful UK start-up agencies and was rated as a UK top 10 public affairs company (Marketing) after only 3 years.

Consolidated's public affairs team is one of the leading exponents of integrated public affairs and PR in the UK. The public affairs team works seamlessly with the consumer and corporate teams to implement fully integrated, cost-effective campaigns. It also specialises in campaigning, CSR, litigation support, political crisis management, reputation management, alliance building and government relations. Specialist discipline areas include Financial Services, Transport, Media and Telecoms, Gaming, Pharmaceuticals and NGOs.

To give a flavour of the diversity of the work conducted by the team, they have advised on the Cullin Inquiry following the Paddington tragedy, launched Stonewall's Election Manifesto 2001, advised the Co-operative Insurance Society on its CSR communications and launched the high profile 'Illegal Weapons in the UK' report for the Countryside Alliance's Campaign for Shooting.

Services offered include: political lobbying; political monitoring; political PR; regulatory work; and litigation support.

Consolidated is a member of the APPC, the PRCA and the Institute for Ethical and Social Accountability. Ed Vaizey is on the Board of Management of the APPC and Jim Boyd is Vice-Chair of the PRCA's Public Affairs Committee. Both are involved in ensuring that the APPC/PRCA Code of Practice for public affairs practitioners are incorporated and understood throughout the Public Affairs and PR industries.

CSM Parliamentary Consultants

Address	72 A Rochester Row
	London
	SW1P 1JU
Telephone	020 7233 9090
Fax	020 7233 9595
E-mail	info@csmparl.co.uk
Website	www.csmparl.co.uk
Staff	4
Chairman	Eric Koops FCA
Managing Director	Christine Stewart Munro
Board Members	Arthur Butler
	Rosemary McRobert OBE
	Robert Lintott
Year of Formation	1974
Trade Body Membership	Christine Stewart Munro is Vice-Chairman of the IPR's Government Affairs Group
Code of Conduct	'No payments have ever been made to MPs, Peers or public officials'

Company Information

Managing Director, Christine Stewart Munro, described as a 'political junkie' by MPs and colleagues, is one of the pioneering Parliamentary consultants in the UK. Since founding CSM in 1974 she has built up a wealth of contacts spanning all the political parties and areas of influence and is recognised for her knowledge of the mechanics of Government.

CSM Parliamentary Consultants are renowned for their in-depth research and tailor made briefs. They pride themselves on diluting relevant information into digestible portions in the knowledge that companies do not have the time to wade through oceans of paperwork. CSM provide a highly competitive value-added information service that keeps companies up to speed on all political developments. It is applicable to organisations that already have a public affairs team and works in sync with in-house teams, or as an outhouse specialist.

An independent consultancy with all-graduate staff, CSM was founded in 1974 to keep companies, trade associations and professional bodies closely in touch with the activities of Parliament and Whitehall.

De Havilland Public Affairs

Address	South Quay Plaza II
	183 Marsh Wall
	London
	E14 9SH
Telephone	020 7517 2200
Fax	020 7517 2233
E-mail	dehavilland@dehavilland.co.uk
Website	www.dehavilland.co.uk
Staff	65
Chairman	Adam Afriyie
Managing Director	William Bracken
Year of Formation	1997
Trade Body Membership	Some staff are members of the NUJ

Client List

Clients include blue chip companies, trade unions, trade associations, charities, campaign organisations and government agencies.

Company Information

The De Havilland service is one of the UK's most comprehensive political, governmental and broadcasting monitoring services, which is continually updated in real time as new information becomes available.

De Haviland brings together everything there is to know about public affairs in one database direct to your desktop (the system is accessed via the Internet);

- You select only the information that you want to see and that is relevant to you;
- The information is continually being updated, refreshed and individually indexed;
- Each customer is allocated an account manager constantly contactable by freephone or e-mail;
- Use mailmerge to communicate directly with specified politicians or journalists;
- Identify future anniversaries or events for future planning.

The Services:
- InfoStream: Live feed developments customised to relevancy for customer (UK & Europe)
- InfoPool: Accessible pool of historical information
- PeoplePoint: Profiles and biographies
- MediaPoint: UK media contacts in the national, regional, local and trade press
- Schedule: Comprehensive list of forthcoming events and anniversaries
- User Contacts: Flexible contact management system

Sources include Governmental, Political, Parliamentary, European, Legislative, Newsdesk and Public Domain, Broadcast Reports and Devolved Affairs.

DLA Upstream

Address	3 Noble Street
	London
	EC2V 7EE
Telephone	020 7796 6574
Fax	020 7796 6139
Website	www.dla.com/upstream
Staff	17
Chairman	Lord Clement-Jones OBE
Managing Director	Lionel Stanbrook
Director, Campaign Communications	Steve John
EU Public Affairs and Regulatory Counsels	Mike Pullen
	Birgit Ris
Account Director	Kevin Craig
Senior Policy and Information Executive	Suzy Awford
Account Executives	Kajsa Stenstrom

Stuart Thomson

Agnieszka Charkiewicz

Year of Formation	1999
Estimated Fee Income	c. £1m
Parent Company	DLA
Brussels Office or Affiliate	DLA Upstream (Brussels)
Trade Body Membership	DLA is regulated by the Law Society of England and Wales and the Law Society of Scotland. Some staff are members of the IPR.

Code of Conduct

DLA Upstream has adopted a Code of Practice which is included in all employee and client contracts:

We will act at all times in good faith and in an honest manner towards clients and the institutions of government and public bodies, with proper regard to the public interest.

In particular we will:

- Always disclose the identity of our client in making representations to public authorities and will identify ourselves by name and by firm
- Never withhold information from the institutions of government, subject to normal considerations of commercial confidentiality
- Use our best endeavours to pursue client requirements, subject to the obligation to advise clients where objectives may be illegal, unethical or contrary to professional practice; and to refuse to act for that client if requested to act in such a manner
- Satisfy ourselves of the honesty and accuracy of any statements made both to clients and to public authorities by or on behalf of our clients;
- We will provide consultancy services in an honest manner In particular we will not
- Disseminate false or misleading information knowingly or recklessly and shall exercise proper care to avoid doing so inadvertently
- Sell for profit to third parties copies of documents obtained from public institutions;
- Permit any professional conflicts of interest
- Engage in any practice or conduct in any manner detrimental to the reputation of DLA or the legal profession in general;
- We will at all times act properly towards public representatives and institutions. In particular we will not
- Save for entertainment and token business mementoes, offer, give or cause a client to give, any financial inducement or other inducement to a representative or employee of any elected body or to any public servant or official or person acting on their account.
- Receive any incentive (whether from a client, supplier or would-be supplier to the company or elsewhere) that could be construed in any way as a bribe or solicitation of favour.
- Propose or undertake any action which would constitute an improper influence;
- Pay any retainer or commission to an MP, MSP, AM or MEP;
- Exploit public servants or abuse the facilities in institutions of central and local government or fail to con-

duct ourselves in accordance with the rules of the Palace of Westminster and the European Parliament while within their precincts

Any of our directors or staff who may at any time be in the position of an elected representative or a member of the House of Lords will at all times observe the appropriate codes of conduct or rules applying to the institutions of which they are members.

Company Information

DLA Upstream is the public affairs and communications arm of the law firm DLA. DLA Upstream is unique in combining the legal experience and proven infrastructure of one of Europe's leading law firms, with in-depth communications and public affairs expertise across the UK and EU. The established City legal practice is reinforced by a network of UK regional offices, as well as offices in Brussels and Hong Kong, and D&P offices across Europe.

By bringing together public affairs and communications with the law, DLA Upstream's clients benefit from a 'new depth of knowledge' which other public affairs firms are unable to provide. DLA Upstream utilises the sectoral expertise and understanding of DLA's lawyers in delivering a tailored package to its clients. DLA Upstream can fully involve specialist lawyers when required. Bringing public affairs and law together strengthens the position of the client.

The DLA Upstream model of public affairs is more akin to that operating in Brussels and Washington DC. Public affairs firms in the UK have traditional developed as part of PR firms - this makes DLA Upstream fundamentally different from its competitors. DLA Upstream has built an impressive list of clients since its inception in a range of sectors - financial services, utilities, transport, healthcare, advertising and e-commerce

The DLA Upstream team brings together a number of individuals with a wide scope of experiences. In particular, DLA Upstream offers a number of services to clients such as:

- Early warning of public policy developments, with concomitant strategic advice and analysis
- Advance intelligence on key policy issues and personalities
- Advocacy for policy and legislative change
- Competition and regulatory advice
- Campaign strategy and development of your case
- Crisis management
- Fully integrated UK/EU public affairs and legal advice
- Media - strategic advice on dealing with the media at all levels (and journalist meeting programmes)
- Advice on drafting and amending legislation at both EU and UK level
- Contact building and networking

DLA Upstream has extensive expertise in media relations, campaigning and policy research and intelligence. Its specialists concentrate on e-commerce, health, financial services, retailing, utilities, environment, property and planning. DLA Upstream's rapidly expanding team has been recruited on the basis of academic excellence as well as professional experience, with backgrounds that include business, law, advertising, trade associations, academia, print and television journalism and the civil service.

Edelman Public Relations Worldwide

Address	Haymarket House
	28-29 Haymarket
	London
	SW1Y 4SP
Telephone	020 7344 1200
Fax	020 7344 1222
E-mail	bernard.hughes@edelman.com
Website	www.edelman.com
Staff	135
UK Chief Executive	Tari Hibbitt
UK Chairman	Nigel Whittaker
UK Managing Director	John Mahony
Director of Corporate and Public Affairs	Stuart Smith
Director of Public Affairs	Bernard Hughes
Associate Director	Cathy Byrne
Account Directors	Jeremy Browne
	Alex Bigg
Senior Account Manager	Suzanne Kyle
Account Managers	Sarah Jane Gray
	Rob Mallows
Senior Account Executives	Eleanor Conroy
	Lucy Thom
Account Executives	James Tait
	Emma Meehan
	Jodie Fielder
	Amy Kitson
Year of Formation	Edelman London, 1967;
	Edelman PR Worldwide, 1952
Estimated Fee Income	£11m
Brussels Office or Affiliate	Edelman Brussels
Trade Body Membership	PRCA; CBI; many staff are members of the IPR
Code of Conduct	A 'Vison, Mission and Values' statement is available that applies to all divisions across the Edelman company.

Company Information

Edelman PR Worldwide was established in Chicago in 1952, and is the largest independent and fifth largest public relations firm in the world. The company now has 41 wholly owned offices and employs 2000 people worldwide servicing a wide range of local and multi-national clients. Edelman's London office was founded in 1967 and was the company's first venture outside the USA.

Edelman's convergence approach means that their clients are not restricted to traditional public affairs services alone. Most of Edelman's clients will need to mobilise, at various times, capability from business-to-business, corporate reputation, product marketing, technology specialists, and consumer marketing. Teams are developed according to client needs and work together to benefit their clients.

Staffed by former advisers for all three main political parties, journalists, media experts, civil servants, policy advisers and experienced public affairs practitioners, Edelman's public affairs offering is provided by a team with extensive experience of advertising companies and other organisations. Edelman Public Affairs provides a range of services including: strategic counsel; campaign strategy and implementation; political monitoring and intelligence gathering; political media relations; public policy analysis; parliamentary briefing and lobbying; research, report, submission and speech drafting.

Edelman Public Affairs claims an impressive knowledge of the political media. They maintain daily contact with senior members of the Westminster lobby (both newspaper and broadcasting), providing valuable opportunities to tap into the latest thinking and discuss pro-active media stories. They pride themselves on being able to draw on experience of the sometimes 'arcane' Westminster media processes.

In addition to their consultancy function, Edelman retains a dedicated real-time monitoring unit. Their five-strong team works seven days a week to provide the corporate and public affairs team, as well as the clients, with monitoring and analysis. In addition to covering national newspapers and broadcasts, they offer a specialist ability to scour web-sites with the aim of tracking down relevant information from less conventional sources.

European Public Policy Advisers

Address	25 Green Street
	London
	W1K 7AX
Telephone	020 7399 3450
Website	www.eppa.com
Year of Formation	1987

Client List

Advertising Education Forum; Aventis; Becton Dickinson; Black and Decker; British Horseracing Board; Clean Air; CollectNicad; Consumers Association; Lucent Technologies; Mars Incorporated and Subsidiaries; Port of Rotterdam; SAPA; Vasatek; Worldwide Brands Inc.

Company Information

EPPA has been at the intersection of business, political and social change in Europe since 1987 – a position that gives them equal strength in three critical business disciplines: public policy, corporate social responsibility and change management.

All organisations operating in Europe face challenges arising from regulatory, political and social developments – challenges which can have a big impact on their profitability, reputation, competitive advantage and value. EPPA believe no-one can match their depth of experience or record of success. They are independent and owned by their associates, so they are accountable only to their clients and personally committed to their business. Based in every EU member state capital, Brussels and several Central and Eastern European countries, they intend to be close to the policy-setters, close to their clients and their clients' markets, sensitive to their concerns and fluent in their languages. Their people come from a wide range of government, industry and academic backgrounds and from all over Europe and form tailor made teams for each client assignment.

In EPPA Public Policy, clients are advised on policy & regulatory developments that affect their business in Europe and assist clients in presenting their priorities and concerns to the people who govern their affairs.

In EPPA Consulting, clients are helped to manage the risks and opportunities that arise from evident and emerging political and social changes, making measurable contributions to their clients' business.

EPPA's commitment is to help their clients achieve 'Sustainable Business Excellence' by mastering continuous, externally driven, change. An increasingly important source of that change is 'civil society' and changes in social values and political behaviour. The value of a business is increasingly dependent on its reputation with a diverse set of stakeholders who have a wide variety of frequently conflicting expectations. Trust is hard to build, hard to maintain but easily and very expensively lost. EPPA Consulting works closely to ensure that internal strategic planning accurately foresees and takes sufficient account of changes in this sphere.

Fishburn Hedges

Address	77 Kingsway
	London
	WC2B 6ST
Telephone	020 7839 4321
Fax	020 7242 4202
E-mail	info@fishburn-hedges.co.uk
Website	www.fishburn-hedges.com
Year of Formation	1995
Trade Body Membership	APPC
Code of Conduct	APPC

Client List

Alconbury Developments Ltd, Pearl Assurance, Powergen, Unilever, Bacon and Woodrow, Equal Opportunities Commission, Pre-school Learning Alliance, Relate, Securities and Futures Authority.

Company Information

Since their public affairs practice started in 1995, they have worked on the basis that the public affairs area of communication should be seen in the context of an organisation's overall communications and reputation management. This is particularly so as the UK government and the European Union recognise more than ever the power of public opinion and the media.

Fishburn Hedges offer experience and expertise in Whitehall, Westminster and in the European Union, and they advise on the wider forces which drive the political and corporate agenda, such as consumer groups, pressure groups, think tanks and the media. They see their role as being to help companies and organisations develop their policies, challenge and inform their thinking, and develop and implement communications and public affairs programmes which meet their specific objectives. These might range from government relations and regulatory affairs to campaigning, reactive crisis and issue management to planned corporate positioning, or corporate ethics to corporate community involvement

Their staff are drawn from the civil service, former political advisers, ex-journalists and the voluntary sector. As members of the Association of Professional Political Consultants, they adhere strictly to a code of professional conduct, and both their clients and consultants are registered with the Parliamentary Commissioner for Standards and the Cabinet Office.

Training is a core component of life at Fishburn Hedges, from their formal FhD (Fishburn Hedges Development) programme, to informal "knowledge sharing" workshops and external courses to deepening IT skills.

Flagship Group

Address	140 Great Portland Street
	London
	W1W 6QA
Telephone	020 7299 1500
Fax	020 7299 1550
E-mail	simon.elliott@flagshipgroup.co.uk
Website	www.flagshipgroup.co.uk
Staff (Whole group)	60
Chairman of Flagship Group	Tony Good
Managing Director of Flagship Group	Diana Soltmann
Finance Director of Flagship Group	John Berry

Flagship Board Members and Directors	Simon Elliot
	Graham Johnson
	Dick Newby
Account Director	Charlotte Maxwell-Lyte
Account Executive	Emily Dearden
	Louise Madel
Consultants	Glynes Thornton
Year of Formation	1999; formed by the merger of four companies
Associated Companies	Good Relations India
Trade Body Membership	PRCA: some staff are members of the IPR
Code of Conduct	PRCA

Client List

Current Clients at time of going to print: Pringle Scotland; Astrium Ltd; The Prince's Trust; Millers Insurance Groups; Old Mutual; Terry Farrell Associates; Howard do Walden Estates; The Carribean Banana Exporters Association; Amadeus.

Company Information

The Flagship Group was formed in April 1999 by the merger of The Matrix Partnership, Millbank PR, The Words Group and Fox Presentations.

Gathering, analysing and acting on political intelligence, whether at Westminster, in Brussels, Strasbourg or Whitehall, demands a fine understanding of the inner workings of the corridors of power. Public affairs is a mainstay of Flagship's offering to corporate, institutional or non-profit clients, often in conjunction with other strategic counsel and issues management, sometimes in circumstances which demand crisis management. They have expensive experience of regulatory matters, defence and property-related planning issues.

Foresight Communications

Address	Golden Cross House
	8 Duncannon Street
	London
	WC2N 4JF
Telephone	020 7484 5087
E-mail	email@foresightcomms.co.uk
Website	www.foresightcomms.co.uk
Staff	3
Managing Director	Mark Adams OBE

Research Executive	Daisy Gibbs
Year of Formation	2001
Code of Conduct	Foresight Communications abides by the Code of Conduct of the Association of Professional Political Consultants, although it is not currently a member.

Client List

'Foresight's clients cover a variety of sectors, including IT, utilities, energy, engineering and services. We offer an integrated public relations services, with particular expertise in campaigning and in offering clients advice and support in securing public sector contracts'.

Company Information

Foresight Communcations Ltd is a public relations company, specialising in political consultancy. It was founded in January 2001 by Mark Adams OBE, a former Private Secretary in Downing Street to Prime Ministers John Major and Tony Blair.

Since January, Foresight has built up its client base which now comprises a variety of companies ranging from multinationals through to start-up campaigning organisations. Foresight has managed to grow flexibly around its early success and as a result, is able to adapt its services to the specific needs of its clients. Where necessary, Foresight can draw upon the expertise of partners within the consultancy industry to deliver this services.

Foresight aims to offer clients an unmatched understanding of the public policy making process and this is reflected in the fact that its core team have many years experience at the heart of Government. Its most recent recruit Daisy Gibbs, joined as a Research Executive in April 2001, having worked as a Parliamentary Assistant to Graham Stringer MP, now a Government Whip.

Foresight offer: perceptions and issues audits; political monitoring; strategic counselling; position papers; identification and targeting o key opinion formers; using media relations; event management; researching new developments; developing political action plans for local government and devolved administrations; advice and support on international institutions.

GCI Political Counsel

Address	New Bridge Street House
	30-34 New Bridge Street
	London
	EC4V 6BJ
Telephone	020 7072 4000
Fax	020 7072 4010

E-mail	rcartwright@gciuk.com
Website	www.gciuk.com
Staff	9 political counsel; 200 company wide
Chief Executive	Adrian Wheeler
GCI London: Chief Executive	Sue Ryan
Finance Director and Company Secretary	Claire Dobson
GCI Political Counsel: Director	Rod Cartwright
Associate Director	Alicia Griffiths
Group Account Director	Ian Whitiker
Senior Consultant	Jon Sacker
Account Managers	William Comery
	Stephen Munday
	Charlene White
	Adam Morris
Account Executive	Joanna Nunney
Year of Formation	1999
Estimated Fee Income	£1.3m
Parent Company	GCI Group Inc. - the global public relations subsidiary of Gray Global Group
Associated Companies	APCO UK; The London Communications Company; Pettifor Morrow
Trade Body Membership	PRCA; Director Rod Cartwright is a member of the PRCA Public Affairs Committee; some staff are members of the MSF

Client List

Transport *for* London, Film Council, Motor Neurone Disease Association, Gibb Transport Consulting, Lee Valley National Athletics Centre, London Bus Initiative.

Company Information

GCI Political Counsel provides GCI's clients with advice on parliamentary and government relations, and strategic public affairs advice and guidance across the UK & European political system. Their services are available both on a niche basis and as a fully integrated part of GCI's rounded communications offering.

Their mission is partly to help their clients manage the threats and pitfalls generated by political and public policy change. However, they also assist organisations from all walks of life to capitalise on the commercial and presentational opportunities generated by political developments that are so often overlooked.

The full range of services they provide - from political monitoring, policy analysis and message development to contact management and bid development - is designed to act as an effective management tool. They claim they are more than simply an add-on to other parts of the marketing mix. Reflecting the realities of modern politics, their services focus on both traditional public affairs audiences and the broader political community, which can play a pivotal role in the development of policy.

GCI Political Counsel was established in 1999 as the public affairs practice of GCI London, a top ten public relations consultancy founded in 1987 and owned by Grey Global Group. GCI Political Counsel works jointly with clients of GCI's specialist teams in the City (GCI Financial), healthcare (GCI Healthcare), technology, marketing communications, professional and financial services and business to business, as well as servicing its own public affairs client portfolio.

Golin/Harris Ludgate

Address	111 Charterhouse Street
	London
	EC1M 6AW
Telephone	020 7324 8602
Fax	020 7324 8601
E-mail	cevans@golinharris.com
Website	www.golinharris.com; www.ghl-intelligence.com
Staff	60
Parent Company	The Interpublic Group of Companies
Associated Companies	Allied Communications Group; Golin/Harris
	International; Weber Shandwick
Brussels Office or Affiliate	PRP
Trade Body Membership	APPC
Code of Conduct	APPC

Client List
Bicycle Association; Bryant Homes; Buckingham Securities; McCarthy & Stone Plc; Wates Landmark; Sunley Estates; National Car Parks; John Lewis Partnership; Waitrose; Foster and Partners; Franklin Mint; Hampton Trust; Risk Metrics; SAP; St Merryn Meats; AUTIF; Derbyshire Building Society; Liverpool Victoria; Claims Direct.

Company Information
Golin/Harris Ludgate is a specialist financial and corporate public relations investor, investor relations and public affairs business.

Businesses, organisations and individuals have a message which defines them and is central to their success. It needs to be clear and simple because there has never been a more crowded or a tougher environment in which to get that message heard: increasingly demanding stakeholders, aggressive interrogation and 24 hour news means that the message has to be focussed and communication, robust. Media, politicians, the public, consumers and shareholders are amongst the key stakeholder groups. Golin/Harris Ludgate Public Affairs' message is that they are creative, aggressive and effective – whatever the brief. They pledge to build a platform for their client's message, and shield it. They will be a champion of their client's corner.

Their services are designed to provide individualised solutions to a wide range of communication-led business issues. They work as a stand-alone practice or alongside other advisers and consultants. They work either on retainer or on a project fee basis. Among the services they offer are:

- Strategic Counsel: One to one with senior executives on issues management and advice on developing messages and communicating them effectively.
- Message Development and Media Strategy
- Intelligence and Policy: The Intelligence Unit supports the account teams and clients directly. The Unit is dedicated to analysing the market place, and reflects thinking on a wide variety of policy issues. The Unit keeps place with legislative and parliamentary business.
- Parliamentary Liaison: Golin/Harris Ludgate Public Affairs boasts a track record of delivering and building relationships with decision-makers and those who influence thinking.
- Opinion Polling and Research: Gives a snap-shot of the target audience and its thinking at any given moment in order to test, refine and strengthen the message and its impact on the audience.

Good News Communications

Address	9 Old Queen Street
	London
	SW1H 9JA
Telephone	020 7222 4279
Fax	020 7222 4189
E-mail	cwgoodnews@aol.com
Website	www.goodnewspolitics.co.uk
Staff	5
Managing Director	Chris Whitehouse
Year of Formation	1997
Estimated Fee Income	£300,000

Client List

The British Olympic Association, Sony Broadcast and Professional Europe, The British Health Care Association, Consumers for Health Choice, Holland and Barrett Retail Ltd, The Cambridge Health Plan, The Health Food Manufacturers Association, The Portman Group, The American Soybean Association, Lidl Supermarkets, Teletext Ltd, Talkradio Ltd, The Westminster Media Forum, NRJ Radio, Tara Television, Media Ventures International, The Council for Responsible Nutrition (USA), The Barlow Clowes Investors Group, Bional UK Ltd, FSC Vitamins, Nutricia.

Company Information

Good News Communications is a specialist political consultancy advising clients on how best to identify, approach and influence the key decision-makers of Westminster, Whitehall and Brussels, together with the Scottish Parliament, Welsh Assembly and local Government.

Supported by careful monitoring, research and intelligence gathering, their experience of and involvement in the political life of the United Kingdom and Europe enables them to provide guidance on the development and implementation of strategies to achieve clearly defined objectives. They are not primarily lobbyists or advocates, believing that in most cases their clients are themselves best-placed to articulate their own views from a position of authoritative knowledge of their own business and sector in which they operate.

Part of the Greenhouse Communications Inc. network of international consultants, Good News Communications has access to expertise in countries across the world.

GPC International

Address	Four Millbank
	Westminster
	London
	SW1P 3JS
Telephone	020 7799 1500
Fax	020 7222 5872
Address	GPC Scotland
	3rd Floor
	14 Charlotte Square
	Edinburgh
	EH2 4DJ
Telephone	0131 226 2102
Fax	0131 225 9859
Website	www.gpc.co.uk
Staff	40

Managing Director	Kevin Bell
Vice Chairman and Deputy Managing Director	Ross Degeer
Directors	Richard Marsh
	Julie Harris
Senior Consultants	Imogen Shillito
	Bernard Harrison
	Corrine Pluchino
	Helen Silver
	Nick Richard
	Jules Peck
	Dan Fox
Parent Company	Omnicom
Associated Companies	GPC Scotland
Brussels Office or Affiliate	GPC International
Trade Body Membership	APPC
Code of Conduct	APPC

Client List

3i; Alcan; Alliance Pharmaceuticals; American Pharmaceuticals Group; Annington Homes; Ariba; ASDA Stores; Association of Scottish Colleges; Bank of Scotland; BG Group; BMW; British Airways; British Association of Pharmaceutical Wholesalers; British Music Rights; Channel 4; Cordis; CREATE; Edinburgh Chamber of Commerce; English, Welsh and Scottish Railway Ltd; Ethicon-Endo Surgery; Glaxo Welcome; Imperial Cancer Research Fund; Innisfree/Private Partnerships Forum; Johnson & Johnson; Lattice Group; London Underground; Marks & Spencer plc; Merck Sharp & Dohme Ltd; National Asthma Campaign Scotland; Nirex; Novartis; OTE; Pfizer; Phillips Petroleum; Post Office; Provident Financial; Quintiles; Rio Tinto plc; Roche Diagnostics Europe; Schering Healthcare; Scottish & Newcastle plc; SELECT; SMMT; Stockley Park; TEG; Tesco; The Essentia Group; The King's Fund; Thoroughbred Breeders Association; Transport for London; United Distillers and Vintners; Vauxhall; Vodaphone; WWF; Wyeth.

Company Information

GPC is a Public Affairs and Strategic Communications consultancy with 500 consultants in offices throughout Europe, the USA and Canada. As a leading firm of its kind, GPC is well positioned to assist clients in every major area of government policy and communications strategy across the globe. Through their government affairs practice, they assist clients in a wide variety of specialist areas, including energy, environment, competition, healthcare, technology, trade, and transport. Strategic Communications complements their government affairs advisory and advocacy work to deliver a comprehensive, integrated set of services.

Their Strategic Communications team offers the following services:

• Public Affairs Communications: crisis management, advocacy communications, perception audits, public consultations and community and stakeholder relations.

- Corporate Communications: internal communications, corporate and executive profile building, reputation management and communications management consulting.
- Media Relations: pan-European press outreach, media positioning, training and monitoring, press conference management and materials development and design (media releases, press kits, video news releases, etc.).
- Information Technology and On-Line Services: support and strategic advice for internet start-ups, launching, promoting and developing web sites, extensive extranet services and the latest internet technology.

Grant Butler Coomber

Address	Westminster House
	Kew Road, Richmond
	London
	TW9 2ND
Telephone	020 8322 1922
Fax	020 8322 1923
E-mail	publicaffairs@gbc.co.uk
Website	www.grantbutlercoomber.com
Parent Company	GBC Worldwide
Associated Companies	GBC Conseil

Company Information

Grant Butler Coomber is a public relations consultancy specialising in corporate, business-to-business, consumer and public affairs market sectors.

Since its establishment in 1992, GBC's west London office has experienced rapid yet managed growth. In its first five years, from a zero base, the company has achieved a turnover in excess of £2 million and built up a prestigious portfolio of clients.

GBC UK provides a wide range of services based on high-level consultancy. With a strong foundation in creative marketing, GBC works in synergy with the clients business to develop cost effective campaigns that focus on creativity, added value and return on investment. GBC also prides itself on introducing new ideas to clients, bringing life and energy to well targeted campaigns.

GBC works in synergy with its clients to create a tailored approach to all campaigns and projects. This process invariably leads to strong client relationships with GBC consultants soon coming to be regarded as part of the in-house team.

The Public Affairs team specialise in: identification of target audiences and key messages; national, regional and local campaigns; training and involvement of regional and local employees and volunteers; and storyline developments. They specialise in multi-level lobbying and targeting politicians, organisations, experts, and representatives that are relevant to a client's objectives.

Their Policy Research, Media Monitoring, Campaign Audit teams focus on: research on policy of key political parties, pressure groups and think tanks; daily or weekly monitoring of key stories in selected media - broadcast and press; analysis of existing campaigns and report of results and recommendations.

Harry Barlow

Address	16 Hanson Street
	London
	W1W 6UD
Telephone	020 7436 2701
Fax	020 7580 5838
E-mail	harry_barlow@hotmail.com
Staff	3
Managing Director	Harry Barlow
Finance Director	David Sutton
Company Secretary	Mick Leighton
Year of Formation	1999
Estimated Fee Income	£180,000
Trade Body Membership	IPR

Client List

Mayor of London, Sickle Cell, Taylor Nelson Softie, RNIB, Home Office.

Hill and Knowlton

Address	35 Red Lion Square
	London
	WC1R 4SG
Telephone	020 7413 3049
Fax	020 7413 3113
E-mail	apharoah@hillandknowlton.com
Website	www.hillandknowlton.com

Staff	18 public affairs; 350 company wide
Managing Director	Andrew Pharoah
Board Members and Directors	Sarah Richards
	Simon Miller
Associate Director	Ian Hagg
Account Directors	Alison Phillips
	Lalu Dasgupta
	Dawn Parr
Account Managers	Matt Ball
	Sarah Eden-Jones
Account Executives	David Oliver
	Nick Conway
Designated Research/Monitoring Staff	Chloe Campen
Year of Formation	1927 Worldwide; 1969 UK
Estimated Fee Income	£2m Public Affairs; £25m UK Consultancy
Parent Company	WPP Group Plc
Brussels Office or Affiliate	Hill and Knowlton Int. Belgium
Trade Body Membership	APPC; PRCA; some individuals are IPR members

Code of Conduct

APPC; Also abides by the following pledges:

- We value our integrity foremost and will conduct all our business with our clients, with the media, and with our colleagues in the most ethical manner
- We will listen carefully to our clients and we will learn their businesses in order to serve them well
- We will harness the company's collective knowledge, creativity, and expertise around the world to deliver the best advice and counsel to our clients
- We will consistently monitor our clients' satisfaction with regard to our performance and service, ensuring that we fulfil all commitments
- We will hire, train, develop and retain the best and brightest people in the public relations industry
- As an international company, we will always strive to serve our clients with uniform expertise and consistent service, wherever our clients need us
- We will use all available research tools and market intelligence to develop the right solutions to our clients' needs
- We are committed to investing in state-of-the-art information technology to better serve our clients anywhere in the world
- We will always recognise the contribution made by the people of Hill and Knowlton to our client's success, and we will reward the people of Hill and Knowlton fairly while providing them with career opportunities and professional growth
- We will take pride in and enjoy our work

Clients

Have directly contributed through clients, to: The creation of Channel 5; the privatisation of the UK's modern nuclear electricity generating stations; aspects of the design of Stakeholder pensions, outlawing the bundling of insurance products and mortgages, liberalising the regulatory framework for casinos, securing three cuts in pool betting duty, preserving historic market charter rights, changing broadcasting legislation to secure extra investment for Channel 4.

Company Information

Hill and Knowlton can be distinguished by a number of factors. Firstly, for their 'holistic' approach to public affairs, analysing not only who takes a decision but also who influences the decision makers, directly or indirectly, whether in Brussels, Westminster, Edinburgh, Cardiff, the media, interest and pressure groups or think tanks. Secondly, strategies are formulated and messages are developed that are most likely to meet with a receptive ear and to support a client's advocacy. They also believe that public affairs should be integrated with clients' business strategies, identifying a pro-active policy agenda which is directly related to business priorities. Another emphasis is that through Hill and Knowlton, clients can seek allies, building strategic alliances of supporters to reduce the likely charge of acting through self-interest, and enabling allies to carry the message to key audiences. Lastly Hill and Knowlton believe that the management of corporate reputation and public affairs are closely related. Being seen to make a commercially disinterested but authoritative contribution to policy debate may help an organisation to differentiate itself from competitors and to express its personality and philosophy.

They are the fourth largest PR company in the UK, owned by the WPP Group which also owns Burson-Marsteller and Ogilvy PR.

International Public Affairs

Address	36 Murray Mews
	London
	NW1 9RJ
Telephone	020 7267 6196
E-mail	epdeakins@netscapeonline.co.uk
Staff	1
Year of Formation	1995

Keene Public Affars Consultants

Address	Victory House
	99-101 Regent Street
	London
	W1B 4EZ
Telephone	020 7287 0652
Fax	020 7494 0493
E-mail	kpac@keenepa.co.uk
Website	www.keeenepa.co.uk and www.keenepublicaffairs.co.uk
Staff	9 (plus freelances)
Chairman	Sir Malcolm Thornton FRSA
Managing Director and Chief Executive	Tony Richards
Company Accountant	Noel Yardley
Company Secretary	Albert Levy
Board Members	Tony Richards
	Sir Malcolm Thornton
	Frances Knox
Senior Account Manager	Nick Ryan
Account Manager	Will Dingli
Senior Account Executive	Ruth Prior
Account Executive	Abby Smith
Office Manager	Aureen Ritchie
Year of Formation	1986, wholly owned independent company
	since 1992.
Estimated Fee Income	£550,000
Brussels Office or Affiliate	Euralia SA
Trade Body Membership	IPR

Code of Conduct

The company and its staff, both permanent and temporary, are committed to the following code of conduct in their professional duties:

- To serve clients honestly in a competent and professional manner.
- To maintain the confidentiality of commercial information and data in accordance with agreed contractual obligations.
- To use best endeavours to pursue client requirements, subject to the obligation to advise clients where objectives may be illegal, unethical or contrary to professional practice and to refuse to act for that client

if requested to act in such a manner.

- Save for entertainment and token business mementos, not to offer, give or cause a client to give, any financial or other incentive to a representative or employee of Parliament or to any public servant or person acting on their account; nor to receive any incentive (whether from a client, supplier or would-be-supplier to the company elsewhere) that could be construed in any way as an improper inducement or solicitation of favour.

- To act in good faith in an honest manner towards the institutions of government, public bodies and public servants with proper regard to the public interest.

- To satisfy themselves of the honesty and accuracy of any statements made both to clients and to public authorities by or on behalf of their clients. Where representations are made or produced solely by their clients, to use their best endeavours to counsel and secure honesty and accuracy.

- To disclose the identity of their client in making representations to public authorities.

- Not to withhold information from the institutions of government or their representatives subject to normal considerations of commercial confidentiality.

- Not to hold a pass entitling them to access to the Palace of Westminster as a secretary or research assistant, to avoid abusing the facilities or institutions of central and local government and to conduct themselves in accordance with the rules of the Palace of Westminster while within its precincts.

- Not to engage in any practice or conduct in any manner detrimental to the reputation of the client, consultancy or the profession of political consultancy in general.

Company Information

Keene Public Affairs Consultants is one of the few independent specialist public affairs companies in the UK. It was established by its Managing Director, Tony Richards, in 1986 and was initially part of a group of communications companies specialising in Public Affairs, Public Relations, Marketing and Advertising. This experience is reflected in the core public affairs services Keene currently provides. These include the full range of Government and Parliamentary relations including regulatory affairs but also press relations, crisis management and government marketing. The latter has been developed to help companies participate in public procurement by understanding the political and policy decision-making process.

In 1992 the Company became independent and is wholly owned by its Directors. Many of its original clients are still with the Company – a loyalty that Keene values and nurtures. An integral part of its approach is to promote its clients - not itself - by providing dedicated, tailor-made services with a strong ethical bias.

The Company's staff are drawn from all the political Parties, providing a balance of perspective and experience. All client projects are carried out by small teams, selected according to the range of skills required.

Keene's clients include multinational companies, foreign governments, UK and European trade associations and public bodies. The Company and its staff have particular experience in sectors such as aviation and transport, the chemical, metal and mineral industries, education, defence, energy and environmental issues, health and social care, information technology, utilities and public services, travel and tourism,

Keene Public Affairs Consultants offers public affairs services in the UK and the European Union. It has associates in Brussels and Washington and links with public affairs companies in other European Union member states.

Lexington Communications

Address	4 Park Place
	London
	SW1A 1LP
Telephone	020 7898 9002
Fax	020 7898 9252
Website	www.lexcomm.co.uk
Staff	17
Partners	Ian Kennedy
	Michael Craven
Directors	Kate Bearman
	Ann Rossiter
Senior Consultants	Sarah Doyle
	Josie Dobrin
	Nigel Warner
	David Wilson
	Nick Wellington
Consultants	Jacob Bridges
	Harpinder Athwal
	Sara Smith
	David Harris
Year of Formation	1998
Trade Body Membership	APPC
Code of Conduct	APPC

Client List

Accenture; Amerada Hess; Artsworld; Bristol 2008; British Airways; BSkyB; Commercial Radio Companies Association; Daily Mail and General Trust; The Discovery Channel; Dixons; Dow AgroSciences; Fox Kids UK; Granada Media; The History Channel; Intergen; Land Securities Trillium; Metronet; MTV; Nickelodeon; North Oxfordshire Consortium; Novartis; Peel Holdings; The Performance Channel; Powderject; Prudential; J Sainsbury Plc; Serco; Syngenta; Telewest; Turner Broadcasting; Wellcome Trust.

Company Information

Lexington Communications was formed in November 1998 by Ian Kennedy and Mike Craven. Mike Craven was a former managing director of GPC and Ian Kennedy was a former director of GPC. They were joined at the start by ex-GPC senior consultants Kate Bearman and Sarah Clancy. The company's focus since the start has been to provide high-level strategic political and media advice to major corporations. Lexington takes an issues based approach to client briefs. Picked as public affairs 'Consultancy to Watch' by *PR Week* publication in 1999, Lexington is now one of the largest independent public affairs and communications consultancies with average fee income growth of over 50%.

Client successes include the high profile and successful media and political campaign against proposals for an additional digital licence fee. On this campaign, Lexington worked for a consortium of commercial broadcasters including BskyB, Granada, Ondigital and Carlton. Lexington also worked for Granada Media in their successful bid for United News and Media which gained the approval of the Competition Commission. Lexington advise Metronet, picked as preferred bidder for three of the underground lines under the current government PPP.

Nick Wellington joined from Stephen Byers' private office at the DTI in 2000 and media specialist Josie Dobrin joined from Luther Pendragon at the end of 2000. Recent recruits include David Wilson, ex-special adviser at DETR and Nigel Warner, former special adviser at the Cabinet Office. Ann Rossiter, former director at Fishburn Hedges, joined in September 2001.

LLM Communications

Address	Bugle House
	21A Noel Street
	London
	W1F 8GR
Telephone	020 7437 1122
Fax	020 7437 7788
E-mail	llm@llm.co.uk
Website	www.llm.co.uk
Staff	22
Managing Director	Ben Lucas
Finance Director	Karen Fuidge
Directors	Jon Mendelsohn
	Neal Lawson
	Craig Leviton
	Olly Grender
Account Managers	Clara Bentham
	Mark Titterington
	Henneke Sharif
	David Abrahams
	Hugh Simpson
Senior Account Executive	Sean McKee

Account Executive	Phil Avery
Researcher	Daniel Leighton

Year of Formation	1997
Estimated Fee Income	£2m
Trade Body Membership	APPC
Code of Conduct	APPC

Client List

The Accident Group, Alodis, AWG Plc, Atticus, Boots Plc, Capita Plc, COLT Technologies, Compaq, Corillian, The Edexcel Foundation, Federation Electronic Industries, Finance & Leasing Association, Focus Housing Association, Freshwater, Fund Managers Association, GlaxoSmithKline Plc, Ineos, iSoft, KPMG, Ladbrokes, Local Government Association, Manchester City Council, Merrill Lynch Investment Managers, Nationwide Building Society, News International, National House Building Council (NHBC), National Housing Federation, Office Angels, Official Payments, Orange, Parents Gateway, People PC, Policyholders Protection Board, Prisma, RSPCA, Shelter, Teramedia, Town & Country Finance Interest Groups, Value Retail Plc.

Company Information

LLM Communications is a strategic communications consultancy specialising in public affairs advice to major companies, trade associations, public and voluntary sector bodies. They deliver services to their clients in terms of monitoring, intelligence, contact programmes and policy analysis.

The changing relationship between Government and organisations has been put into sharp focus by New Labour. This is a Government that was swept into power by its understanding of the media and public opinion and continues to be swayed decisively by both. Now that the genie of public accountability is out of the bottle - no matter who is in Government - the decision-making process will increasingly require the ability to influence both the media and public opinion.

This is a complex, fast moving and unpredictable world that requires public affairs advice based on an understanding of the dynamics of complex relationships between different stakeholder groups.

It means that while Westminster may remain the apex of decision making, the route to influencing it lies as much in the media, pressure groups, think tanks, local campaigns, other stakeholders and popular mobilisation as in direct contact with politicians. LLM Communications understands this fast developing world and has successfully helped organisations to adapt to it.

Core Services: Information Monitoring and Analysis; Strategic Advice; Contact Programme Development; Parliamentary affairs; Policy analysis and forecasting; Corporate communications; Manifestos / Brief Preparation; Campaigns; Working with others

Specialist services: Communications Strategy Unit; Regulatory and Compliance Issues; Stakeholder relations; Reputation and communication audits.

LOBBYcontact from Campaign Information

Address	Shuttleworth Centre
	Old Warden Park
	Biggleswade
	SG18 9DX
Telephone	01767 626910
Fax	01767 626919
E-mail	info@lobbycontact.com
Website	www.lobbycontact.com
Chairman	Rhion Jones
Director	Elizabeth Gammell
Technical Consultant	Christopher Greetham
Sales Consultant	Stacey Jones
Year of Formation	1988
Parent Company	Campaign Information Ltd
Brussels Office or Affiliate	Anna MacDougald - EU Public Affairs

Company Information

LOBBYcontact from Campaign Information, the UK's leading provider of political databases and Relationship Management IT systems, offers clients a powerful combination of up-to-date political information and a professional contact management system.

It is designed specifically for companies and organisations wanting to influence key decision makers. Clients can track complex relationships with opinion formers over time, with greater continuity and control over their long term objectives.

Used by many of the UK's top companies, the biggest Trade Unions and Trade Associations, Campaigning Pressure Groups, Charities, Consultancies and Public Affairs Professionals; LOBBYcontact can be used wherever there is a need for political relationships to be monitored.

With representation in Belfast, Brussels, Cardiff and Edinburgh, the LOBBYcontact family of political databases now includes; House of Commons; House of Lords; London Assembly; Whitehall; Scottish Parliament; National Assembly for Wales; Northern Ireland Assembly; Oireachtas; European Parliament, and European Commission.

Luther Pendragon

Address	21 Whitefriars Street
	London
	EC4Y 8JJ
Telephone	020 7618 9100
Fax	020 7355 1078
E-mail	post@luther.co.uk
Website	www.luther.co.uk
Year of Formation	1992
Chairman	John Booth
Associates	Michael Brunson
	Sir Kenneth Warren
Non-Executive Directors	John Preston
	Nicholas Taylor
Partners	George Pitcher
	Ben Rich
	Andrew Sharkey
	Charles Stewart-Smith
	Simon Whale
	David Wheeldon

Company Information

Luther Pendragon offers strategic communications consultancy and tactical implementation to a wide variety of clients. It draws on the journalistic, business, financial and political backgrounds of its senior consultants to integrate otherwise separate disciplines. Luther Pendragon is an issues-led consultancy. This means that an understanding of the issues affecting a client must come first. This issues-led, integrated approach to communications has enabled Luther Pendragon to target an increasing proportion of public affairs business.

Luther Pendragon's approach is based upon offering a clear understanding of how public policy is derived, together with effective research skills and high quality political intelligence. Luther believes that the role of the public affairs consultancy is to equip clients with facts, information and well-mustered arguments, attuned to the Government or key decision-makers. It recognises that politics does not exist in a vacuum and, under New Labour like never before, the media heavily influences policy.

The political and public backgrounds of Luther Pendragon consultants enable them to offer an integrated approach to Public and Parliamentary affairs, bringing influence to bear through integrated, effective and ethical campaigning to the benefit of an increasing number of clients.

Morgan Allen Moore

Address	104-110 Goswell Road
	London
	EC1V 7DH
Telephone	020 7253 0802
Fax	020 7253 0803
E-mail	london@morganallenmoore.com
Address	Morgan Allen Moore Wales
	First Floor, Bay Chambers
	West Bute Street
	Cardiff
	CF1 6GH
Telephone	029 2046 1610
Fax	029 2046 1617
E-mail	wales@morganallenmoore.com
Website	www.morganallenmoore.com
Directors	Steve Morgan
	Shelley McNicol
	Richard Moore
	Jo Welch
Year of Formation	1998
Parent Company	AUR Communications Group
Associated Companies	SFS Events Management

Company Information

Morgan Allen Moore provide a comprehensive political and public relations service across a broad range of sectors. They believe that traditional public affairs programmes often falter because they fail to take into account the inter-relationships that can exist between commercial climates, political developments and media presentation. They recognise the importance of these inter-relationships and are skilled at developing mechanisms that use them to the best advantage of their clients. They specialise in changing thinking; client development; coalition building; crisis management.

The UK operation spans Hansard and media monitoring to integrated political and media campaigns, with offices in London, Cardiff and the South East and targeted support from Brussels. Their monitoring service is based on an 'intelligent' system, customising all material so that the clients receive only pertinent material and do not have to waste time monitoring the monitoring. All appropriate material on agreed subject areas is faxed by mid-morning, and a regular report providing an overview of developments is also compiled on a daily/week-ly basis as appropriate. All material is prepared in a report style with political analysis explaining the background to the issues.

Morgan Allen Moore Wales, headed by Jo Welch, offers strategic advice, helping to form productive partner-ships with the National Assembly, thereby ensuring Clients have a real opportunity to achieve their aims and objectives. The Cardiff Bay-based research team offers one of the most comprehensive monitoring services available in Wales, providing coverage of all Assembly Business including chamber debates, written and oral questions, consultations and statements.

Newspoint Agency

Address	Clutha House
	10 Storeys Gate
	London
	SW1P 3AY
Telephone	020 7222 8040
Fax	020 7222 6943
E-mail	info@newspoint.co.uk
Website	www.newspoint.co.uk

Company Information

The Newspoint Agency are an officially accredited News Agency, based in the Press Gallery of the House of Commons. Within their website they provide a full range of services ranging from Parliamentary news to a comprehensive monitoring service.

Their 'Early Warning Daily Diary' is one of the most important and widely used features of their services. They also offer a 'Lunchtime Update', a Weekly Wallguide, as well as monitoring of all the select committees, GLA Coverage and parliamentary monitoring.

Opinion Research Business

Address	9-13 Cursitor Street
	London
	EC4A 1LL
Telephone	020 7430 0216
Fax	020 7430 0658

E-mail	gheald@opinion.co.uk

Staff	7

Year of Formation	1994
Estimated Fee Income	£1.1m

Company Information

The Opinion Research Business was established in 1994 by Gordon Heald, former Managing Director of Social Surveys (Gallup Poll). The company delivers research of the highest quality in both the quantitative and qualitative fields. They understand that opinion research is a crucial tool in developing new market strategies, conducting industry analysis and guiding policy making decisions. The Opinion Research Business has experience in the design and execution of surveys in a number of specialised fields, foremost among these are public affairs and public opinion polling (including studies personally conducted for the President/Prime Ministers of nine countries).

Parliamentary Bookshop

Address	12 Bridge Street
	London
	SW1A 2JX
Telephone	020 7219 3890
Fax	020 7219 3866
E-mail	bookshop@parliament.uk
Website	www.parliament.uk

Company Information

Located off Parliament Square, the Parliamentary bookshop specialises in all documents relating to the business of Parliament including Stationary Office and Government publications.

Parliamentary Contacts Consultancy

Address	Suite 49, 34 Buckingham Palace Road Belgravia
	London
	SW1W 0RH
Telephone	020 7639 8249

Fax	020 7277 9221
E-mail	Mendora@parliamentarycontacts.com
Website	www.parliamentarycontacts.com
Staff	3
Directors	Lord Philip Howard of Penrith
	Mr Tim Kendall
Year of Formation	2001
Estimated Fee Income	Not trading
Parent Company	Parliamentary Contacts Recruitment Agency

Client List

Victim's Voice, The Big Issue (London)

Company Information

Parliamentary Contacts was launched immediately after the June 2001 General Election by Mendora Ogbogbo and has so far gained positive support from all political parties. In September 2001 the company launched its political consultancy arm during the Party political conference season, making Ms Ogbogbo, the first black woman in Britain to run a Public Affairs company. Parliamentary Contacts Consultancy now provides charities, single-issue pressure groups and trade unions with a professional parliamentary consultancy service and has already gained interest from major clients within the charity sector. The consultancy will provide smaller charities and pressure groups with the additional opportunity to interface directly with politicians and the parliamentary process. The company has a large number of contacts, hence its name. Its staff contains people from all social backgrounds and contains professionals who have worked directly for charitable organisations and so are acutely aware of the difficulties such groups face in trying to get their issue on the political agenda.

Parliamentary Monitoring Services

Address	19 Douglas Street
	London
	SW1P 4PA
Telephone	020 7233 8283
Fax	020 7821 9352
E-mail	info@parliamentary-monitoring.co.uk
Staff	12

Year of Formation	1979
Subsidiary Companies	PMS Publications

Client List

PMS provides monitoring and research services on a confidential basis to public relations and public affairs consultancies, companies, charities, trade associations, QUANGOs and diplomatic missions.

Company Information

Parliamentary Monitoring Services Ltd is an independent company dedicated to attaining and delivering the highest standards in monitoring, research, intelligence and publishing.

The company started in 1979 as a division of the Media Information Group. In 1984 it became an independent limited company, and in 1989 it bought the Parliamentary & EEC News Service. In 1991 it formed its own publishing company, PMS Publications.

Monitoring services cover Westminster and Whitehall, the new Scottish Parliament and Welsh and Northern Ireland Assemblies, and the European Union. Information is gathered and disseminated in hard copy, by fax and by e-mail. News services are delivered by e-mail and broadcast FAX. There are four regular bulletins a day, plus a number of weekly and 'flash' bulletins. A range of databases are available on disk, on CD-ROM, or via the internet. They cover the House of Commons, the House of Lords, the Scottish Parliament, the Welsh and Northern Ireland Assemblies, and the European Parliament. Biographical data and contact details are included, and the databases operate as powerful search and mailing tools.

Perchards

Address	Drover House
	16 Adelaide Street
	St. Albans
	AL3 5BH
Telephone	01727 843277
Fax	01727 843193
E-mail	info@perchards.com
Website	www.perchards.com
Staff	4
Founding Directors	David Perchard
	Denise Perchard
Political Affairs Manager	Pat Murtagh
Research Affairs Manager	Gill Bevington
Year of Formation	1987

Company Information

Perhcards was founded in 1987 as a specialist public affairs consultancy to monitor and assess legislative developments at national and EU level and to help private-sector clients adopt politically aware corporate policies.

David Perchard has been involved with packaging waste management policy ever since the European Commission began taking an interest in the environmental impact of packaging in 1974. The consultancy has expanded its interest in recycling and waste management to cover electrical and electronic products, end-of-life cars and batteries as the EU has developed 'producer responsibility' policies for these sectors. Perchards are expert in both EU policies and policy-making procedures and in national policies across the 18 countries of the European Economic Area. They are also retained by some clients to track and report on general legislative issues at the EU and national level. Perchards monitors regulatory policies, analyses the implications, plans strategy and helps clients put the message across. Furthermore, some clients retain Perchards to help them press for changes in proposed legislation. For Perchards, effective lobbying means awareness and understanding of the political agenda, identification of the key players, the ability to transform technicalities into clear briefs, a sense of timing and a reputation for integrity and credibility as a source of reliable information.

Their in-house translation service produces reports in English from a variety of sources in other languages.

The Policy Partnership

Address	The Studio
	51 Causton Street
	London
	SW1P 4AT
Telephone	020 7976 5555
Fax	020 7976 5353
E-mail	tpp@policypartnership.com
Website	www.policypartnership.com
Staff	7
Chairman	Lord Paddy Gillford
Managing Director	Andrew Smith
Director	Rory Scanlan
Head of Research	Sarah Mindham
Research Analyst	Charlie Napier
Year of Formation	1993 (Originally Westminster Policy Partnership)
Estimated Fee Income	£800,000
Trade Body Membership	APPC; CBI
Code of Conduct	APPC

Client List

British Borneo Oil & Gas Plc; British Car Auctions; BT Plc; Government of Azerbaijan Republic; Government of the State of Bahrain; Keyspan Energy Development Corporation; Inkatha Freedom Party; London Greenways; Philip Morris Ltd; Ramco Energy Plc; Towry Law; United Parcel Services; Yukos Oil.

Company Information

The Policy Partnership is a leading public affairs consultancy based in Westminster offering a flexible range of public affairs solutions. Believing that a good way to structure the process of solving the client's problems is through understanding them, often a public affairs audit is taken. This considers the client's objectives and evaluates the in-house resources already in place to meet them. Then The Policy Partnership is able to advise on a suitable strategy, drawing on the following disciplines:

- Public policy analysis and research: political monitoring of the latest news; media monitoring and news gathering; legislative tracking; political intelligence, insight and evaluation; issues research; qualitative and quantitative polling; web crawling and internet monitoring; daily/weekly reports.
- Reaching the opinion formers: strategic advice and support; message development; briefing programmes; contact building and networking; advocacy and third-party representation; coalition building and alliances; grass-roots campaigning; drafting reports and submissions; corporate citizenship; event management and sponsorship; press and public relations.
- Public affairs training: public policy workshops; select committee training.

The Policy Partnership has defied the trend for the smaller independent consultancies to sell to larger groupings. All accounts are headed up at Director level and this has enabled the company to build on an impressively solid client base. Originally focussed on the energy sector, The Policy Partnership is now believed to offer public affairs solutions to a much broader range of organisations. Sectors represented include transport, financial services, consumer goods, environmental and governmental. Primarily offers all public affairs services, but has recently shown an increasing emphasis on media relations, with very strong links with the international press corp.

Political Intelligence

Address	23 Palace Street
	Westminster
	London
	SW1E 5HW
Telephone	020 7233 7377
Fax	020 7233 7294
E-mail	info@political-intelligence.com

Website	www.political-intelligence.com
Staff	18
Managing Director	Nicholas Lansman
Account Director	Michelle Dow
	Jamie Holyer
Year of Formation	1996
Brussels Office or Affiliate	Political Intelligence (Belgium)
Trade Body Membership	IPR

Client List

Internet Service Providers Association (ISPA), Inktomi Clicksure, Internet Watch Foundation (IWF), LINX, Cable & Wireless Global Mobile, European Internet Service Providers Association, Penton Europe, Internet Policy Development (IPD).

Company Information

Political Intelligence is a young and dynamic public affairs company which specialises in providing top-quality regulatory affairs intelligence for the Internet, telecommunication and IT sectors. With experienced consultants in Westminster, Brussels and Madrid, they are able to provide a comprehensive monitoring, intelligence and strategy services on both a national and European level.

Political Intelligence offers a one-stop shop for companies requiring both Westminster and Brussels monitoring, intelligence and lobbying. The majority of laws being implemented in the UK are the result of legislation first introduced by EU institutions and it is sometimes there that decisions need first to be influenced and encouraged.

Regular monitoring and intelligence as well as political expertise and strategic advice is also offered. Information by itself, if not analysed carefully, can often do more harm than good. Their team will scrutinise new policies, consultation documents and raw data to ensure threats and opportunities are not missed or overlooked.

All contact with clients and main activity is carried out by one or more of their senior consultants, and as well as political know-how, the team is fluent in English, French, German, Spanish and Italian. The guiding policy is one of partnership, working with clients in order to bring them the results they need. They believe that as a small company they can provide a service that is both broad in its scope and yet specifically tailored and responsive to their clients' unique needs.

Political Perceptions

Address	12 St Paul's Road
	Richmond
	Surrey
	TW9 2HH
Telephone	020 8940 1248
Fax	020 8940 1238
E-mail	r.rugman@btinternet.com
Managing Director	Roderick Rugman
Year of Formation	1987

Politico's Bookshop

Address	8 Artillery Row
	London
	SW1P 1RZ
Telephone	020 7828 0010
Fax	020 7828 8111
E-mail	bookshop@politicos.co.uk
Website	www.politicos.co.uk
Associated Companies	Politico's Publishing; Politico's Design

Company Information

Politico's bookshop is Britain's only specialist political bookshop, stocking a wide range of political and parliamentary books as well as think tank publications and political ephemera. The breadth and depth of the bookshop's range is surpassed only by the general knowledge of its employees. The sister company of Politico's Bookshop is Politico's Publishing, the publisher of this directory.

Politics Direct

Address	10 Greycoat Place
	London
	SW1P 1SB
Telephone	020 7960 6010
E-mail	info@politicsdirect.com
Website	www.politicsdirect.com
Year of Formation	1999
Associated Companies	Lovelacemedia; Peyser Associates Inc; Stratagem

Client List

Alliance & Leicester plc; Allied Domecq PLC; The Association of Colleges; AIESEC; The Commonwealth Local Government Forum; earthport; East Dunbartonshire Council; Genient; Global Internet Billing (GIB); HotPartners.com; Local Government Association; mondus; Network Lettings; The Society of Black Lawyers; One 2 One; World Online.

Company Information

PoliticsDirect.com monitors all available sources of information relevant to the client. This includes parliamentary publications, Government departments, political parties, think tanks, trade associations, and pressure groups. Information can be mailed, faxed or preferably e-mailed to the client with analysis of its importance and relevance. PoliticsDirect.com holds regular meetings with clients to discuss the latest political developments, examine how future political activities will impact on their company, and help devise plans for future activity. They also provide clients with 24-hour access to their consultants. A political audit offers clients a valuable insight into how they are perceived by key opinion formers. They claim it also provides a valuable evaluation tool if carried out before and after a public affairs programme or a campaign. PoliticsDirect.com offers a free initial consultation via their website for companies who have an issue or problem that may require public affairs consultancy.

Politics International

Address	Greencoat House
	Francis Street
	London
	SW1P 1DH
Telephone	020 7592 3800

Fax	020 7630 7283
E-mail	pi@politicsint.co.uk
Address	1-3 St Colme Street
	Edinburgh
	EH3 6AA
Telephone	0131 220 8210
Fax	0131 220 8310
E-mail	mail@scottish-solutions.co.uk
Website	www.politicsint.co.uk
Staff	20
Managing Director	Andrew Dunlop
Finance Director and Company Secretary	Lesley Gilbert
Board Members	David Massingham
	Amanda Cunningham
Political Consultants	Josh Arnold-Forster
	Alison Cairns
	Pippa Clarke
	Clare Cox
	Stephen Edwards
	Andrew Fletcher
	Sarah Gibson
	Jeannette Gould
	Lisa Poole
	Guy Rainbird
Consultants	Tim Bird
	Rodney Brooke
	Brian Cavanagh
	Rob Hughes
	Fionnulala Jay O'Boyle
	Ross Martin
	John Pierce
	Geraint Price-Thomas
	John Raine
Designated research or monitoring staff	Jo Burgess
	Kate Symons
	Katie Wyglendacz
Year of Formation	1991
Estimated Fee Income	£1.4m

Subsidiary Companies   Scottish Solutions, see APPC

Brussels Office or Affiliates   PRM Consultants Ltd, Houston Consulting Europe

Politics International has exclusive relationships with PRM Consultants and Houston Consulting that complement and support their own European public affairs work undertaken in London. Both are independently owned Brussels based specialist political consultancies. PRM offers a full range of lobbying and government relations services. Houston Consulting specialises in financial service sectors.

Trade Body Membership   APPC; some staff are members of GMB

Code of Conduct

Politics International will act in the best interests of clients at all times, providing best advice and assistance in a manner consistent with this Code.

* Within the context of the company's obligations to clients, Politics International retains the right to act in accordance with its own professional standards.
* Politics International and its staff will use their best endeavours to ensure that clients' positions are represented fairly to Government institutions and other audiences.
* Politics International and its staff will use its best endeavours to ensure that information for Government institutions and other audiences is accurate.
* Politics International will conduct its relations with Government institutions in a transparent manner. Staff will therefore identify themselves as employees of Politics International when in contact with officials, MPs and other audiences If requested, Politics International staff will normally disclose the specific client in whose interest they are working except where commercial confidentiality has been requested.
* Politics International and its staff will ensure that intelligence provided to clients and potential clients is to the best of its knowledge both accurate and proportionate.
* In the course of its professional work, Politics International and its staff will seek access to decision-makers or opinion formers only on the basis of matters of substantive current or potential policy interest. Politics International and its staff will not employ personal, moral or financial pressure to gain privileged access.
* Politics International and its staff will not misrepresent themselves to gain access to Parliamentary or Government institutions' buildings or papers.
* Politics International and its staff will abide by any rules and ethical standards determined by Government institutions.
* Politics International will not provide financial support for party political initiatives.
* Politics International's staff will not be required to work on projects that have objectives which are inimical to their personal consciences.
* Politics International staff will be required to abstain from any political activities which either conflict, or could be construed to conflict, with their work on behalf of Politics International and its clients, or which risks bringing the company, its clients or the political consultancy profession into disrepute.
* Politics International staff will maintain client confidentiality, and will not communicate commercially sen-

sitive, corporate information to other parties without clients' permission.

• Politics International will ensure that its staff are fully aware of the provisions and implications of this Code of Conduct so that they may pursue their duties in compliance with it. We agree to be bound by the provisions of the above Code, which applies to all employees.

Client List

Air Tanker, Association of Investment Trust Companies, Association of Retired Persons Over 50, Association of Technology Staffing Companies, Britannic Money, British Association for Biofuels and Oils, BCP Ltd, British Market Research Association, Careers Management Group, Chemical Industries Association, Cory Environmental Ltd, Energy from Waste Association, Energy Power Resources Ltd, Equitable Life, Euromet Ltd, Forecourt Stores Association, Game Conservancy Trust, General Healthcare Group, Intermediary Mortgage Lenders Association, Kensington Mortgage Company, Lockheed Martin, London Waste, Montedison, OveArup, Property Market Reform Group, Royal Marines, Severn Waste Services, St John Ambulance, Trees for London, Two Way TV, Virgin Atlantic Airways Ltd, Vosper Thornycroft, Wellcome Trust, Westminster City Council.

Company Information

Politics International was founded in 1991, with the expressed intention of bringing a new dimension to public affairs in the UK. The principles upon which the company was founded included a rigorously ethical approach; in-depth understanding of clients and their priorities; acute awareness of the commercial implications of political and public policy decisions and professionalism.

The company has grown to a staff of around 20. Their clients range from blue chip companies to trade associations and charities in a number of different industry sectors. They are particularly proud that they are still working for their first ever clients, the Association of Investment Trust Companies and Vosper Thornycroft.

Politics International provides strategic advice and support to clients on all aspects of public policy, from national legislative initiatives to locally contentious projects. The company has particular strengths in a number of sectors, including environment, energy, planning, defence, transport, financial services, consumer & retail and health.

Politics International has established over the last few years a number of specialist practices that complement their core public affairs services:

Local Solutions and Scottish Solutions deal with issues surrounding local and devolved decision making. They employ a network of external consultants based around the UK, most of whom are former local authority chief executives, who they commission on a project basis to augment their in-house resources.

The Competition & Regulation Practice offers advice to clients involved in mergers and acquisitions or who operate in highly regulated industries. This practice advises clients on pan-European as well as UK deals. Their Procurement Support Practice has a long history of helping companies maximise the commercial opportunities associated with government procurement.

They also have a Communications Practice that helps clients manage their strategic communications. It offers clients a full issues management service, stakeholder and communications audits, business writing and the production of other communications tools, and advice on a range of strategic public relations services.

Portcullis Research

Address	3/19 Holmbush Road
	London
	SW15 3LE
Telephone	020 8789 2798
Fax	020 8879 0795
E-mail	info@portcullisresearch.com
Website	www.portcullisresearch.com
Year of Formation	1989
Estimated Fee Income	£750,000
Associated Companies	Advance Communications
Brussels Office or Affiliate	P&P Partners

Code of Conduct

'Portcullis Research is dedicated to the ethical conduct of Government relations. As professionals, we pledge that we will neither initiate nor take part in any actions which could result in damage to clients' reputations.'

Company Information

Portcullis Research was established in 1989 in a bid to provide an ethically sound Government relations service. They believed that sooner or later a demand would exist for a consultancy in which more than lip service was paid to the notion of ethics.

In particular, clients would benefit from effective services without running the risk that they would subsequently be embarrassed by an association with their Government relations adviser. Their existing clients understand the benefits that flow from their approach and they are particularly proud of their client retention record.

Research can be highly cost-effective, affording opportunities to tackle Government-related problems before they become major crises, using the methods of fire prevention rather than those of the fire brigade. A pound spent on timely research is usually worth ten spent on launching a life-saving lobbying campaign. Portcullis Research is committed to raising lobbying standards. With many years' experience in Government relations practice, working on behalf of blue-chip clients, they have established a reputation for producing precise, accurate information, accompanied by well-argued analysis, well-developed representations and highly effective campaigns.

In turn, Government welcomes carefully-researched, well-analysed, tightly argued and well-presented representations because better information produces better decisions.

Portcullis Research provides a full range of Government relations services and advice encompassing UK and EU political institutions. Clients are enabled to address a wide variety of political audiences through a range of appropriate media, including via the Internet. Helping clients both to exploit opportunities and confront threats, services are delivered electronically, or according to client preference, and include: a political monitoring service for the UK and EU, political advocacy, political research and analysis and political audit.

For Portcullis, political advocacy involves: lobbying Government and advising on case development; advising on the feasibility of clients' lobbying objectives; advising on the building and timing of clients' representations to Government; identifying the precise targets to whom representations should be addressed; assisting in making representations to Government, either directly by the client organisation or acting on behalf of the client.

PPS Group
Incorporating PPS (Local and Regional) Limited and PPS (Public Affairs) Limited

PPS Public Affairs Limited

Address	69 Grosvenor Street
	London
	W1X 9DB
Telephone	020 7493 6077
Fax	020 7493 5730
E-mail	richard.mollet@ppsgroup.co.uk

PPS Local and Regional Limited

London Address	69 Grosvenor Street
	London
	W1X 9DB
Telephone	020 7629 7377
Fax	020 7629 7514
E-mail	nick.keable@ppsgroup.co.uk

Edinburgh Address	12 Alva Street
	Edinburgh
	EH2 4QG
Telephone	0131 226 1951
Fax	0131 226 1957
E-mail	dan.smith@ppsscotland.co.uk

Manchester Address	66/67 Barton Arcade Chambers
	Deansgate
	Manchester
	M3 2BJ
Telephone	0161 832 21393
Fax	0161 834 2744
E-mail	keith.butterwick@ppsmanchester.co.uk

Bristol Address	9 North Court
	The Courtyard
	Woodlands
	Almondsbury
	Bristol
	BS32 4NQ
Telephone	01454 275630
Fax	01454 275 636
E-mail	charles.stgeorge@ppsgroup.co.uk
Birmingham Address	Vienna House
	International Square
	Birmingham International Park
	Bickenhill Lane
	Solihull
	B37 7GN
Telephone	0121 767 1863
Fax	0121 767 1869
E-mail	harriet.kerr@ppsgroup.co.uk
Cardiff Address	Sophia House
	Cathedral Road
	Cardiff
	CF11 9LG
Telephone	029 2066 0194
Fax	029 2066 0198
E-mail	cathy.owens@ppsgroup.co.uk
Website	www.ppsgroup.co.uk
Group Managing Director	Stephen Byfield
Managing Director (PPS Local & Regional)	Nick Keable
Group Director	Charles St George
Director	Richard Mollet
Group Finance Director	Julia Clark
Non-executive Chairman PPS Group	Terry Roydon
Non-executive Director	Keith Byfield
Associate Director (London)	John Mills
Associate Director (Edinburgh)	Dan Smith
Associate Director (Cardiff)	Cathy Owens
Associate Director (Manchester)	Nick Carrell

Associate Director (Birmingham)	Harriet Kerr
Associated Companies	Cherton Enterprises (Belfast); Cabinet Stewart (Brussels)
Trade Body Membership	APPC; PRCA
Code of Conduct	APPC

Client List

ACF Sevenoaks; Alfred McAlpine Homes, AMEC, Arcot Consortium, AROC Ltd., Ballymore Properties, Barratt Homes, Bass Developments, Bath Racecourse, Beazer Homes, Beazer Strategic Land, Belgrave Lane, Berisford Property Development, Berkeley Homes, Boots Properties, British Gas, Bryant Homes, Callington Estates, Capital & Providence, Capital Shopping Centres, CDC, Chartwell, Cheale Meats, Coln Gravel Co, Countryside Alliance, Crest Strategic, David Wilson Estates, David Wilson Homes, Delta (UK) Land Development, EMC Computer Systems, English Partnerships, Gazeley Properties, GHP Group, Granchester Group, Grosvenor Estates, Halifax, Hanson Waste Management, Howard Holdings, JS Developments, Kilmartin Properties, La Salle Investment Management, Laing Homes, Laing Hyder, Leech Homes, Lex Services, Linden Homes, Lostock Pharmacy, Lucas Aerospace, Management Consultants Association, Mariposa, MBH Partnership, McDonalds Restaurants, Meat & Livestock Commission, MEPC, Morrisons, Natwest Properties, National Power, Net-Tel, Orange, Permission Homes, Phillip Morris, Railtrack Property, Redland, Robert Turkey Associates, Roseberry Homes, Ross Jayne & Co, Sainsbury's Supermarkets, Scottish Metropolitan, Sellar Property Group, Shanks Waste Management, Shell Services International, St George Homes, St James Homes, Stannifer Developments, Swan Hill Homes, Taywood Homes, Thames Water, The Pelham Group, Thornfield Developments Ltd, Ushers Brewery, Walton Group, Wates Homes, Weber McGinn, Weatherall Green and Smith, Whitecliff Properties, Wickes, Wilcon Homes, Woolwich, Woolworths.

Company Information

The PPS Group comprises specialist PR and public affairs companies which allow clients to influence every level of UK and European Government, from local councils to the Council of Ministers.

PPS Public Affairs is active in the institutions of the EU, UK central government, the Scottish Parliament and the Welsh Assembly. PPS Public Affairs is a national company with regional capability and an international reach. It claims to bring a new dimension to public affairs, with a firm focus on campaigning, strategic public affairs, and public policy analysts. It is staffed by those who have worked at senior levels in business and government, and who have the experience to work in partnership with clients to add value to their businesses. PPS offers businesses a competitive edge by providing communications advice, public affairs support and political and policy insights. They claim to demonstrate an understanding of clients' needs and business objectives and help with the delivery of key messages to opinion-formers, decision-takers and the networks that influence them.

PPS Local and Regional advises on presenting to local and regional government and community campaigning. All politics is local, and to influence local government – to secure planning permission for a major development, to sell services to local councils or to change local government policies – PPS Local and Regional offer their services. With over a decade of experience in presenting complicated cases to local and regional government, they have particular expertise in helping win planning permission.

PPS Scotland opened in May 1997 and was the group's first presence outside London. PPS Scotland has worked in most mainland local authority areas and has an acknowledged understanding of the councils from Aberdeenshire to Dumfries and Galloway. The new political landscape in Scotland is having a significant impact on all aspects of the country's commercial life. PPS is advising a range of clients on the implications of the new Scottish Parliament.

PPS North, based in Manchester, opened in 1998. It has already established itself as a leading regional player in the field of community campaigning, local government affairs and media relations. The team believe their success is based on their in-depth local knowledge, political insight and extensive experience of issues of management for the property and development industries. Tailor-made and carefully targeted communications campaigns are the focus of the team's work. The breadth of PPS North's expertise ranges from organising small local community relations exercises to spearheading major political lobbying campaigns.

PPS' Bristol team prides itself on its claim to provide high quality advice on local government affairs, community relations and issues management in Wales and the South West. The region served by the Bristol office is particularly sensitive for the development industry. The high concentration of vigorous environmental protest groups and affluent retirees can lead to even relatively straight-forward proposals being transformed into political 'hot-potatoes'. The team has a wide client base, ranging from FTSE 100 companies to small private developers. The company has extensive experience of working on retail, housing and urban regeneration projects, as well as on major mineral extraction schemes.

PR21

Address	67-69 Whitfield Street
	London
	W1T 4HF
Telephone	020 7436 4060
Fax	020 7255 2131
E-mail	jonathan.hopkins@pr21.com
Website	www.pr21.com
Staff	50 (company wide)
Chief Executive	Beverley Kaye
Finance Director	Bobby Lane
Director of Public Affairs and Board Member	Jonathan Hopkins
Account Directors	Joe Brice
	Nick Tennant
Account Executives	Nicola Garrett
	Lorraine Hutchines
	Chris Roberts

Year of Formation	2000; previously the Rowland Company, formed 1961
Estimated Fee Income	£5m
Parent Company	Edelman Worldwide
Brussels Office or Affiliate	Affilitate to the Edelman Group
Trade Body Membership	APPC; PRCA; CIM; IPR
Code of Conduct	APPC

Client List

BT, National Youth Agency, National Endowment for Science, Technology and the Arts, Tobacco Alliance, National Union of Teachers, Scope, Hepworth Building Projects, Hero, London Institute, Philip Lawrence Awards (Home Office), Schering Healthcare, Times Supplements Ltd.

Precise Communications

Address	Laser House
	Waterfront Quay
	Salford Quays
	Manchester
	M5 2XW
Telephone	0161 874 5700
Fax	0161 888 2242
E-mail	preciseinformation@precisegroup.co.uk
Website	www.precisegroup.co.uk

PricewaterhouseCoopers

Address	Plumtree Court
	London
	EX4A 4HT
Telephone	020 7213 5308
Fax	020 7213 4409
E-mail	chris.lowe@uk.pwc.global.com
Website	www.pwcglobal.com
Staff	150,000 company wide

Company Information

PricewaterhouseCoopers, the world's largest professional services organisation, helps its clients build value, manage risk and improve their performance in an internet-enabled world. The firm's public affairs consulting activity provides advice to clients on understanding, responding to and influencing public policy change. They work with top management in the corporate, public and voluntary sectors to develop and implement strategic communications programmes on a wide variety of fiscal, economic, social and regulatory policy issues. They have particular experience in the field of tax policy.

Probus BNW

Address	32 Old Queen Street
	Westminster
	London
	SW1H 9HP
Telephone	020 7340 6480
Fax	020 7340 6490
E-mail	info@probusbnw.com
Website	www.probusbnw.com
Founding Directors	Alastair Bruce
	Gerry Wade
Other Staff	Beth Ginsburg
	Simon Stanley
Advisory Board	Anna Coote
	Martin Findlay
	Clive Landa MBE
	Sir Leonard Peach
	Usha Prashar CBE
	Tony Travers
Year of Formation	1999

Code of Conduct

We will always act in accordance with the highest ethical and legal standards, and with equal opportunities principles. We will follow both the letter and the spirit of recommendations made by the Committee on Standards in Public Life.

- We will produce work of consistent high quality in terms of its appearance, appropriateness, timeliness and value. Our goal is to set standards for best practice in corporate reputation.
- We will handle client information and relationships with the utmost discretion. We recognise that our own best interests lie in satisfying those of our clients.

- We will meet agreed targets for cost, for timing, and for deliverables.
- Through our network of associates we will provide the skills and experience required to meet our clients' needs. We will not accept work for which we cannot offer the necessary expertise.
- We will seek regular evaluation of our work from all our clients. Wherever possible we will establish measurable performance criteria; we will undertake measurement activities and respond to their findings.
- We will avoid unnecessary work, both on our own behalf and that of our clients.
- If any service we provide fails to live up to the commitments in this Charter, we will cancel the fees for that service, in full and without question.

Company Information

Probus BNW emerged out of Bruce Naughton Wade in 1999. Bruce Naughton Wade was formed in 1991. In over a decade of public affairs management consultancy, much of Bruce Naughton Wade's work reflected strong demands from business in three areas: striking the right balance between answering market and societal demands; juggling increasingly complex external relationships; and managing internal changes in corporate structure. With most of their clients being private businesses, Probus BNW emerged as a consultancy specialising in corporate reputation management.

Their ACID Test service enables several companies to assess the level of their preparedness for the change of government in four areas: their awareness of policy developments and key policy actors; their Contacts with relevant players in government and public policy; their management of Issues; and their internal Direction of public affairs activity to protect and promote their business interests. The ACID Test provides companies with an assessment of their strengths and weaknesses and a set of clear recommendations to build on in these areas.

Profile Communications

Address	31 Great Peter Street
	London
	SW1P 3LR
Telephone	020 7654 5600
Fax	020 7222 2030
E-mail	mail@profilecc.com
Website	www.profilecc.com
Chairman	Tom Ross OBE
Executive Directors	Susan Eastoe
	Asifa Vanderman
Year of Formation	1981
Parent Company	Profile Corporate Communciations
Associated Companies	Saltaire (Scotland)

Code of Conduct

'Profile Corporate Communications was established in 1981. Since that time it has never remunerated any MP for services to the company or its clients. We do not believe that it is either necessary or appropriate in the provision of an effective lobbying service. Our philosophy is to build our contacts and knowledge in a low-profile manner which provides value to our clients but does not compromise our professionalism'.

Company Information

Profile Corporate Communications Limited is a privately owned company specialising in managing relationships so that all stakeholders are woven in to their inclusive communications approach. Their guiding principle is that effective communications means an effective organisation.

In addition, Profile provides a full-stream European service encompassing monitoring, intelligence and contact-building covering the European Commission and European Parliament.

Public Affairs Company

Address	21 Otley Road
	Leeds
	LS6 3AA
Telephone	0113 2780211
Fax	0113 2780214
E-mail	pac@publicaffairsco.com
Website	www.publicaffairsco.com
Staff	4
	Geoffrey Lawler
	Nathan Fossey
	Fiona Turner
	Simeon Morris
Year of Formation	1991

Code of Practice

The Public Affairs Company does not engage, and never has engaged, directly in lobbying on behalf of clients, but instead advises clients on how they may most effectively lobby for their interests. We know from experience on both sides of the fence that the client is always the best advocate.

- We will ensure that there is no conflict of interest in our work for various clients.
- All reasonable steps are taken to ensure that all information is accurate and that no false of misleading infor-

mation is knowing disseminated.

- We have never made any payments of offered inducements, of any kind, including entertainment, to an MP or Peer for any reason, and that will continue to be our policy. We do not retain consultants in a paid or unpaid capacity, nor have we in the past.
- We do not use the services of anyone ostsnsibly employed in the Houses of Parliament as a researcher or secretary to an MP or Peer and who as has security pass to that effect.

Client List

Corporate: Association of Coal Mine Methane Operators, Findel plc, Manufacturing Institute, The Webb Group Ltd, UK Coal plc. Pressure Groups and Charities: British Epilepsy Association, Diabetes UK, Finningley Airport Network, National Kidney Federation. Local Government: City of York Council, West Yorkshire Passenger Transport Executive. Education: CollegeNet, NCFE, University of York. Professional Bodies: Aromatherapy Organisations Council, Hairdressing Council, Standing Conference of Principals.

Company Information

The Public Affairs Company was established in 1991 as a specialist government relations consultancy based in the north of England. Since then it has worked with clients spread across the country with often around half of its clients being based in London or the south.

It provides services offering a comprehensive monitoring and analysis of all activity in Government, parliament, political parties, policy groups and other organisations influential in the political process. Its advocacy service researches and prepares strategies to enable clients to achieve their objectives at local or national Government level. It assists with the implementation of those strategies and monitors results to ensure that the programme is working. The Company was founded on the basis that it would not be a lobbyist, but would instead advise clients on how best may present their case and provide them with the necessary intelligence and support to do this.

Through this approach, the Company has over recent years been involved with a number of successful campaigns including the statutory registration of chiropractors, amendments to various government bills, securing increased government grants and developing contact programmes to improve decision makers' understanding of the issues and the work of different organisations.

Although not specialising in particular areas, recently the Company has been particularly involved in education, lifelong learning, health, energy and regulatory issues. Following the re-organisation of the structure of the governance of local authorities, the Company has provided training to local authority scrutiny committee members, cabinet members and other officers.

Priority in their work is given to results being gained, an ethical and professional approach and competitive fees which offer good value. They prefer to offer a flexible arrangement to clients which means not tying them into fixed retainers but working project basis. This approach makes their services accessible to many organisations, particularly charities and education institutions, who otherwise would unlikely be able to afford professional assistance with their dealings with politicians and officials.

Quadrant

Address	63 Cowbridge Road
	Cardiff
	CF11 9QP
Telephone	029 20 237333
Fax	029 20 237444
Address	Millbank Studios
	4, Millbank
	London
	SW1P 3JA
E-mail	enquiries@quadrantpr.co.uk
Website	www.quadrantpr.co.uk
Partner	Peter Duncan

Company Information

Quadrant boasts years of experience in working with local and national politicians, including the briefing of senior Government Ministers. A number of Quadrant staff have worked for local and central government, both in Wales and in Whitehall. The offer a political intelligence service that keeps clients informed of National Assembly and UK Parliament business and how it may affect them.

They can:

* Help clients achieve a better understanding of the role of the new National Assembly for Wales and how it impacts on their business
* Provide early political intelligence of potential changes affecting their clients' areas of interest
* Assist clients in preparing suitable briefing material
* Advise on public enquiries, hearings and other statutory meetings.

Peter Duncan, the partner for Quadrant, was responsible for setting up the Welsh Development Agency's press and public relations unit, and worked as a principal press officer in Whitehall.

Quiller Consultants

Address	11–12 Buckingham Gate
	London
	SW1E 6LB
Telephone	020 7233 9444
Fax	020 7233 6577
E-mail	stapely@quillerconsult.co.uk
Staff	5
Year of Formation`	1998

Company Information

Quiller is a deliberately small, independent and discreet high level issues management consultancy, working to defend and maintain the reputations of major organisations and individuals where the impact of politics, the media, social issues or the law could give rise to high-profile exposure. Their clients include large corporations, professional firms and institutions, foreign governments and some senior individuals. They have a small team of senior consultants, no juniors and work across all disciplines, having had top level experience in the relevant sectors. Their founders – Jonathan Hill CBE and John Eisenhammer spent some time in a major communications consultancy having, in Jonathan's case, been Political Secretary to the Prime Minister in No. 10, and in John's case been Financial Editor of *The Independent* (previously European Editor). Sue Stapely is a practising solicitor, whose previous careers have included being a director of Fishburn Hedges, currently No. 1 corporate communications consultancy, Head of Public Relations at the Law Society, a partner in a law firm, campaigner, parliamentary candidate and BBC Television programme maker. George Bridges MBE was a leader writer with the Times, also worked at No. 10 and ran communications for On Digital when it was first set up. They have no website or marketing materials at present as the majority of work they do for their clients is highly confidential and comes to them by recommendation.

Randall's Parliamentary Service

Address	5 Hobart Place
	London
	SW1W 0HU
Telephone	020 7235 2999
Fax	020 7235 4999

E-mail	info@parliamentonline.co.uk
Website	www.parliamentonline.co.uk
Staff	6
Partners	Patrick Robathan
	Chris Tuohy
Consultants	Heather Randall
	Richard Warmisham
	Nick Allen
Year of Formation	1976

Company Information

Established in 1976, Randall's Parliamentary Service are specialists in parliamentary monitoring. Their service covers Westminster, Whitehall, the Scottish Parliament and the Welsh and Greater London Assemblies. Randall's also offers an unique web-based monitoring service which enables clients to receive their entire monitoring package via the Internet. They do not get involved in lobbying.

Rees and Freres

Address	1 The Sanctuary
	Westminster
	London
	SW1P 3JT
Telephone	020 7222 5381
Fax	020 7222 4646
E-mail	enquiries@1thesanctuary.co.uk
Website	www.reesandfreres.co.uk

Company Information

Rees and Freres are parliamentary agents and act for a number of both local authorities and district councils throughout England. Whilst a number of the projects have a commercial content they also deal with internal local government issues covering all areas of mainstream areas of local government and administrative law. For example:

• Town Centre redevelopment, economic development and urban regeneration schemes.
• Statutory powers, requirements and constraint
• Public Private Partnership and PFI

- Capital and Revenue finance issues
- Local authority interests in companies and other external bodies.
- European, lottery and other domestic funding
- Public Procurement and competition for contracts
- Judicial Reviews
- Public inquiries and statutory agreements for planning compulsory purchase highways and environmental issues
- Transport and Works Act orders
- Major contracts with the private and other public bodies.

They have significant experience of promoting and petitioning against Private and Hybrid Bills. This is a procedure in which tactics and knowledge or procedure is vital and the help of a Parliamentary Agent is essential.

RGMR Media and Government Relations

Address	609 The Chandlery
	50 Westminster Bridge Road
	London
	SE1 7QY
Telephone	020 7721 8750
Fax	020 7721 8749
E-mail	info@rgmr.co.uk
Website	www.rgmr.co.uk
Staff	5
Managing Director	Aidan Relf
Account Directors	Manuela Cregan
	Justina Cruickshank
Year of Formation	1996
Trade Body Membership	IPR
Code of Conduct	IPR

Company Information

RGMR, an independent consultancy specialising in media and government relations, was established in October 1996. Success in public affairs and PR in partnership with clients include:

- Securing a significant allocation of radio spectrum from the Government for a mobile phone network in the face of fierce competitor opposition;
- Assisting a major US insurer in obtaining a licence to carry on business in the UK;
- Securing amendments to recent education legislation in the face of initial Whitehall opposition;
- Obtaining annually Europe-wide media coverage for a European Commission supported conference in Brussels;
- Receiving press recognition of a major improvement in the media's perception of a client over a twelve month period;
- Obtaining extensive national press coverage of the launch of a Government training programme.

Client experience covers a wide range of sectors including financial services, energy, engineering, business competitiveness, transport finane, B2B internet, broadcasting, petro-chemicals, minerals, local government, planning, education and training, major conferences for the OECD and European Commission, healthcare and telecommunications. It also includes running a national press office on behalf of a major client.

RGMR's online opinion-former interviews attract media attention. Politicians interviewed include Patricia Hewitt and Ruth Kelly. Aiden Relf, RGMR's founder and managing director, was previously a senior consultant at two leading agencies, Burson-Marsteller and Citigate Dewe Rogerson.

Saltaire Public Affairs

Address	Saltaire Court
	20 Castle Terrace
	Edinburgh
	EH1 2ET
Telephone	0131 473 5444
Fax	020 228 1222
E-mail	Pamela.Stewart@saltirepr.com
Website	www.saltairepr.com
Director	David Nash
Business Development Director	Kareen Ryden
Assistant Directors	Pamela Stewart
	Hazel Moffat
Researcher	Fiona Burns
Year of Formation	1998
Parent Company	Shepherd and Wedderburn
Associated Companies	Profile Communications

Company Information

Saltire Public Affairs is the public affairs division of Shepherd & Wedderburn WE, one of Scotland's leading commercial law firms with offices in Edinburgh and Glasgow. Established in January 1998 in response to the profound changes in the Scottish political environment, the team at Saltire Public Affairs offers a comprehensive range of services tailored to meet your requirements.

An understanding of the policy and law making process – and their legal context – is an essential tool for individual businesses in seeking a competitive edge or in maximising opportunities. It is equally essential for trade organisations, professional bodies and pressure groups seeking to further their interests in the new Scottish public policy environment.

With their legal and public expertise, they offer help to achieve client's objectives. Effective participation is crucially dependent on communicating with key decision makers at the right time and in the right manner. Saltire claim their skills and experience qualify them to take the lead in this process.

Stormont Strategy

Address	The Red Barn
	47 Whiterock Road; Co Down
	Killinchy
	BT23 6PT
Telephone	028 9754 1899
Fax	028 9754 1890
E-mail	info@stormontstrategy.co.uk
Website	www.stormontstrategy.co.uk
Staff	5
Managing Director	Richard Gordon
Year of Formation	1998
Estimated Fee Income	£175,000
Sister Company	Gordon Corporate Communications Ltd.
Associated Companies	Westminster Strategy (non-exclusive)
Brussels Office or Affiliate	Grayling Political Strategy
Trade Body Membership	APPC; some individuals are member of MIPR
	and NIGAG
Code of Conduct	APPC

Client List

Northern Ireland Parades Commission, Countryside Alliance, Halifax, General Medical Council, National

House Building Council, Norbrook Laboratories, Lagan Developments, Rockport School, Business for Sterling.

Company Information

GCC Stormont Strategy was founded by Richard Gordon and has established a prestigious client base and a very sound reputation for performance. It is well respected by local politicians and officials, and by all print and electronic media with whom close contact is maintained. They are accustomed to dealing with, on the one hand, highly sensitive and high profile issues in the voluntary and public sectors together with more competitive commercial requirements of the manufacturing and service sectors of the economy.

The establishment of the Northern Ireland Assembly, with full legislative powers in most areas of social and economic policy, represents an exciting and challenging time. GCC Stormont Strategy define the issues, help frame the debate and develop clear, consistent and compelling messages. They can clarify the process, identify key players, pinpoint where any potential challenges may lie and establish how best to influence those who matter in an honest and persuasive way.

Few organisations have identical problems and priorities, so services are customised to meet individual needs. It may be that a simple monitoring and intelligence service is required. At the other end of the spectrum, a business may be facing a severe challenge that requires a comprehensive Government and media relations programme.

Services include:

- Research on, and analysis of, the relevant political issues of the day
- Early warning of forthcoming legislation and major policy initiatives
- Carefully researched identification of key decision makers and policy influencers
- Advice and assistance on the content and presentation of case
- Strategic advice on the most effective means of approaching decision-makers
- Help in creating strategic alliances and working with third parties
- Preparation of Assembly Committee appearances
- Support for political briefing and contact building activities

Stratagem

Address	Carnegie Library
	121 Donegall Road
	Belfast
	BT12 5JL
Telephone	028 90 872800
Fax	028 90 972801
E-mail	ideas@strategem-ni.com

Website	www.stratagem-ni.com
Staff	5
Chief Executive	Quintin Oliver
Account Directors	Katherine McDonald
	Peter MacLennan
Account Executive	Terence McErlane
Year of Formation	1998
Estimated Fee Income	£300,000
Subsidiary Companies	Politics IQ - political database management
Associated Companies	Referendum Company Ltd - advises on and
	fights campaigns

Client List

Action Cancer, Age Concern, Arts Council of Northern Ireland, Barnardo's (NI), Belfast City Council, Belfast European Partnership, Belfast Regeneration Office, British Medical Association (NI), CBI Northern Ireland, Health Network, Deloitte and Touche, Diabetes UK (NI), Eastern Health Board, Eastern Health Council, Energy Savings Trust, Focus on Children (NI), Federation of Small Businesses, Friends of the Earth UK, Forum Europe, Health Finance Managers Assoc., Institute of Health Managers, Institute of Public Health, International Council for Social Welfare, Marks & Spencer, Mencap (NI), National Lottery Charities Board (NI), Northern Ireland Film Commission, National Energy Action, Northern Ireland Electricity, Northern Ireland GP Forum, One-2-One, Overseas Tourism Marketing Initiative, Pharmacia & Upjohn Ltd, Probation Board (NI), Royal National Institute for Deaf People, Royal College of Nursing (NI), Southern Council, Sports Council (NI), Training for Women Network, Translink, Ulster Cancer Foundation, Vodafone, Westcare, Woodland Trust, Young Enterprise (NI), Youth Council Northern Ireland.

Company Information

Stratagem was formed by Quintin Oliver in the summer of 1998 to assist various bodies, whether in the private or the public sector, to get their issues on the agenda of the Northern Ireland Assembly, the North-South Ministerial Council, the Civic Forum or the Council of the Isles. He is joined by Peter MacLennan, a former politician and research assistant during the multi-party talks at Stormont and Katherine McDonald who worked for Labour in Opposition; returning to Northern Ireland in 1997 she has worked as press officer for a large criminal justice organisation. Stratagem offers professional advice and support in the areas of monitoring, information and research, and lobbying.

Monitoring: Offers a comprehensive monitoring service, studying and filing the transcripts of all Assembly sessions and of committees and other public hearings. Also monitor the North-South body and the Council of the Isles.

Information and Research: Maintains records on the Northern Ireland civil services, on the newly elected Assembly members and on the new bodies as they develop.

Lobbying: Organising briefing meetings, delegations and advocacy of the case to all relevant opinion formers. Also advise on appropriate publicity back-up, but often the lobbying is best done privately.

Training and Awareness: Illustrated sessions on new administrative and political structures. Workshops, planning exercises and the art of lobbying explained.

Strategy in Scotland

Address	26 Great King Street
	Edinburgh
	EH3 6QH
Telephone	0131 558 8719
Fax	0131 558 8680
E-mail	info@strategyinscotland.co.uk
Parent Company	Grayling Group (Part of Havas Advertising)
Associated Companies	Strategy Wales; Westminster Strategy
Brussels Office or Affiliate	Grayling Political Strategy

Company Information

Strategy in Scotland, based in Edinburgh, offers a comprehensive range of services to clients with interests in Scotland, who need advice on how best to make a case to the Scottish Parliament. The establishment of the 129-Member Parliament, with legislative and tax-varying powers, has transformed the political debate in Scotland and will have a significant effect on relationships with Westminster/Whitehall and the European Union.

Strategy Wales

Address	First Floor, Regus House
	Flacon Drive
	Cardiff
	CF10 5RU
Telephone	029 2050 4028
Fax	029 2050 4200
E-mail	info@strategywales.co.uk
Parent Company	Grayling Group (Part of Havas Advertising)
Subsidiary Companies Associated Companies	Strategy in Scotland; Westminster Strategy
Brussels Office or Affiliate	Grayling Political Strategy

Company Information

The decisions by the people of Wales, Scotland and Northern Ireland to vote for devolved institutions ushered in the most radical shift of power in the UK this century. The Grayling Group has ensured, through Strategy Wales, that they have an established presence in Wales since the Welsh Assembly began operating. It was the first company of its kind to set up shop in Cardiff. Located in Cardiff Bay, right by the National Assembly, Strategy Wales is run by experienced Welsh political consultants. Wales has its own unique political make-up and set of local institutions. Knowledge of whom to approach and how to approach them, along with the ability to devise a comprehensive strategic overview, is vital to any organisation wishing to move into or expand its operations in Wales or deal with any specific issue.

SWR Worldwide

Address	Aldermary House
	15 Queen Street
	London
	EC4N 1TX
Telephone	020 7950 2118
Website	www.swrworldwide.com
Managing Director, Europe	Phil Riggins
Associated Companies	Weber Shandwick | GJW Public Affairs

Client List

AT&T, Comsat, Blue Cross Blue Shield, PhRMA, Miller Brewing, Schering Plough, National Taxpayers Union, Defenders of Wildlife, Bankruptcy Industry Coalition.

Company Information

SWR Worldwide is a full-service strategic opinion and market research firm that develops research-based solutions to public affairs challenges. For organisations facing challenges driven by legislation, regulation or other public policy factors SWR aims to discover what the public, voters, opinion leaders, 'insiders', or decision makers know and think about them.

Taylor: Bennett

Address	One Duchess Street
	London
	W1W 6AN
Telephone	020 7580 4300
Fax	0207 580 4044
Email	tb@taylorbennett.com
Website	www.taylorbennett.com
Founding Directors	Airdre Taylor
	Annita Bennett
Number of employees	15
Year of formation	1982

Clients List

ABN AMRO, ABI, AMP UK, Astra Zeneca, BBC, Billiton, BP Amoco, British Airways, BT, Diageo, Dixons, EliLilly, Financial Times, General Medical Council, GlaxoSmithKline, Goldman Sachs, Granada Media, HarperCollins Imperial Cancer Research, ING Barings, KPMG Consultants, L'Oreal, Marsh Europe, Nike UK, Orange, Philips Electronics NV, Powergen, Royal Collection, Royal Shakespeare Company, Shell, Siemens, Tate & Lyle, Taylor Woodrow, Transco, Walt Disney TV, Whitbread.

Company Information

Taylor:Bennett is the market authority in corporate communications and public affairs search and selection with an in depth knowledge that distinguishes it from general management headhunters.

Established in 1982 by Airdre Taylor and Annita Bennett, the organisation now comprises six consultants and six researchers including a specialist team dedicated to public affairs.

Strong relationships with clients and candidates have been built by delivering: sound judgement and counsel; real understanding of clients' needs and the related business drivers; total discretion and confidentiality; consistent results and continual refinement of the comprehensive data base.

Tim Pendry

Address	Third Floor
	33 Bury Street
	London
	SW1Y 6AX
Telephone	020 7930 5485
Fax	01892 683984
E-mail	enquiries@timpendry.com
Website	www.timpendry.com
Staff	2
Executive Chairman	Tim Pendry
Managing Director	Jenina Bas
Year of Formation	1998
Trade Body Membership	IPR; Middle East Association

Code of Conduct

We follow best practice guidelines on representation and are transparent as to our interests in dealing with the media, government, politicians and the general public.

Client List

Full lists of recent and current clients, as well as case studies of some of the work that has been undertaken, are available for bona fide business callers contacting our office but are not published. All contracted clients are made aware of other contracted relationships relevant to their case before agreement is concluded.

Company Information

Tim Pendry was founded in 1998 with clients from emerging world community who required public relations, media relations and public affairs in the West. The principals have a long track record both in providing best practice communications consultancy services and in private consulting to significant individuals from the emerging world. Tim Pendry justifiably claims proven experience as a best practice adviser to emerging market interests in the West and as a provider of political campaigns advisory service both in the UK and globally.

Tim Pendry's philosophy of political communication does not emphasise defensive monitoring, infiltration and attempts to control opposition. Instead a broader-based management philosophy is offered based on a proper understanding of participant motivation, on an understanding of power relations and on practical negotiation skills. Operating directly and through associates, they have managed projects such as the El-Shifa case, the Algosaibi Campaign and, currently, the South Iraqi Marshes Project and 'The Middle East in London'. Their European affiliate is Bood & Co. operating from Paris.

Services include: international/UK media relations advice and news distribution; full service public relations project management; political consultancy, advocacy and organisation; issues management; crisis support and campaign management in international relations; intelligence evaluation; European media relations services; Pan-Arabic media relations; a particular understanding of anti-globalisation ideology and organisation.

Vacher Dod Publishing

Address	1 Douglas Street
	London
	SW1P 4PA
Telephone	020 7828 7256
Fax	020 7828 7269
E-mail	politics@vacherdod.co.uk
Website	www.politicallinks.co.uk

Vacher Dod are the publishers of Dod's Parliamentary Companion and the quarterly Vacher's Parliamentary Companion. They also provide online database information on all aspects of Parliament including biographies of politicians and voting records of MPs.

VLP Group

Address	2nd Floor, India House
	45 Curlew Street
	London
	SE1 2ND
Tel	020 7403 7500
Fax	020 7403 6714
E-mail	ianb@vlp.co.uk
Website	www.vlp.co.uk
Number of employees	15
Managing Director, VLP Group	John Levick
Managing Director, VLP Ltd	Sarah Levick
Operations Director	John White
Client Services Director	Sarah Watts
Head of VLP-Government (VLP-g)	Ian Beaumont

Estimated Fee Income	£1 million
Parent Company	VLP Group
Subsidiary Companies:	VLP Ltd
Trade Body Membership:	PRCA, CIM

Company History

VLP was originally formed by Paul Vousden and John Levick in 1990. VLP has recently undertaken an MBO and become the VLP Group following Paul Vousden being bought out and moving on.

VLP-g is the issues and government affairs division of VLP. It is headed by Ian Beaumont, who has over 20 years experience of working in and with central and local government organisations. VLP-g assists its clients in communicating with government in the most effective way possible, utilising their excellent contacts in central and local government departments and organisations. They help clients to get their issues and concerns across; to maximise the value of their contacts with government; and to ensure a continuing positive dialogue across the political spectrum.

VLP-g also provides PR and marketing support directly for government departments and organisations, working on specific campaigns or as part of policy implementation teams. This helps them to keep abreast of government issues and concerns and, where relevant, convey these to their business clients. It's a two way process that benefits both sides. VLP-g also provides an issues and public affairs perspective to other VLP services, such as crisis management, media relations and media training.

The Waterfront Partnership

Address	130–132 Tooley Street
	London
	SE1 2TU
Telephone	020 7787 1200
Fax	020 7787 1201
E-mail	stevebramall@thewaterfront.co.uk
Website	www.thewaterfront.co.uk
Staff	11
Chairman and Managing Director	Nick Finney OBE
Deputy Managing Director	Stephen Bramall
Public Affairs Director	Mark Walker
Head of Communications	Arthur Leathley
Director of European Affairs	John Gansler
Year of Formation	1990

Estimated Fee Income	£1.1m
Parent Company	The Waterfront Group
Associated Companies	The Waterfront Conference Company
Brussels Office or Affiliate	The Waterfront Partnership
Code of Conduct	APPC

Client List

Associated British Ports, Associated British Ports (Southampton), Association of Train Operating Companies, Civil Aviation Authority, ClearWay, Docklands Light Railway, Eurotunnel, Freight Transport Association, Greater Manchester Passenger Transport Executive, GNER, George Hammond plc, Merlin Entertainments Ltd, Merseytravel, National Express Group plc, Regional Airports Ltd, Strategic Rail Authority (European Monitoring Service only), South Yorkshire Passenger Transport Executive, TubeRail, US Airways.

Company Information

The Waterfront Partnership was established in 1990 by Nicholas Finney and Iain Dale, specifically to direct a campaign to secure legislation to facilitate the privatisation of the public trust ports. From this initial success The Waterfront Partnership has developed into the UK's leading public affairs and public relations consultancy specialising exclusively in the transport sector. It now advises a wide range of transport undertakings, from public sector organisations and regulatory agencies, through to leading transport operators, trade associations, manufacturers and equipment suppliers.

The company has witnessed unprecedented growth in the last two to three years, partly due to the growing political interest in transport and the complexity of the issues involved, but also due to the highly specialised nature of The Waterfront Partnership's services. All of the consultancy's senior team enjoyed successful careers in the transport sector before joining the Partnership, whether in business, the Civil Services, the trade union movement, journalism or a political party. This ensures advice that is realistic and relevant to the client's interests, while being supported by a round experience and knowledge of the mechanics of government.

In addition to providing general public affairs and public relations advice to clients, designed to support their day-to-day activities, The Waterfront Partnership increasingly also works on specific assignments and projects rather than simply on general public affairs or public relations activities. Projects are generally related to client's interest in promoting a particular project which might require statutory planning approval, or approval under the Transport and Works Act, or providing support for a client's bid for a public sector contract under the PFI or PPP initiatives.

Alongside the Waterfront Partnership is The Waterfront Conference Company, established in 1993.

Weber Shandwick | GJW Public Affairs

Address	110 St Martin's Lane
	Covent Garden
	London
	WC2N 4RG
Telephone	020 7841 5555
Fax	020 7841 5777
E-mail	nclarke@uk.webershandwick.com
Website	www.webershandwick.com
Staff	London:53; Edinburgh:5; Cardiff:7;
Joint CEOs (Weber Shandwick)	Colin Byrne
	David Brain
Chairman	Wilf Weeks
Managing Director	Nigel Clarke
Senior Directors	Jon McLeod
	Paul Barnes
Finance Director and Company Secretary	David Horne
Directors	David Peel
	Pete Bowyer
	Evie Soames
	Cameron Jones
	Mari James
	Associate Directors Bill Jones
	Hugh Milward
	Jeremy Fraser
	Jim Dickson
	Tony Hutt
	Tony Page
	George Hutchinson
Senior Consultants	Sam Walker
	Jo Nove
	Andrew Mills
	Lee Findell
	Luke Akehurst
	Liam McCloy
	Ben Abbotts
	Nick Wright

	Peter Digger
	David Milne
	Catherine Rose
	Daran Hill
Consultants	Toby Orr
	Sue Daley
	Elizabeth Jackman
	Angela Merron
	Chris West
	Josephine Spiller
	Louise Reilly
	Lucy Shure
	Michael Pooley
	Andrew Henderson
	Tom Griffin

Year of Formation	2001
Estimated Fee Income	£7m
Parent Company	Weber Shandwick Worldwide
Brussels Office or Affiliate	Weber Shandwick | Adamson
Trade Body Membership	APPC; IPR; PRCA
Code of Conduct	APPC

Client List

Over 130 clients which "range from household names from the Footsie 100, to local authorities, trade associations, charities or single-issue campaigns". In London its staff are organised into specialist units. These cover: City and Finance; Competition and Regulation; Local Government and Planning; Health; Defence; Industry; Transport and Construction; Education; and London Government.

Company Information

In October 2001 Weber Shandwick and GJW decided to merge.

The decision made waves in the world of public affairs and public relations, because neither company made the jump from a positon of weakness. By any measure the two consultancies were number one and number two in the field. Weber Shandwick and GJW merged for a single overriding reason: to improve the service their experts offer to people. Their new public affairs consultancy is used by giants like Coca Cola, McDonalds and the BBC; by a range of SMEs; by national governments and local councils; and by a raft of non-governmental organisations. The people already on our books welcomed the merger. Not a single client of Weber Shandwick or GJW elected to leave them as a result of the change. Additional companies and organisations have continued to seek and purchase their services. Weber Shandwick \| GJW has fully staffed offices in Edinburgh, Glasgow, Cardiff, Belfast, Dublin, Manchester and more than 150 countries worldwide. In Brussels, the two most respected public affairs teams were those fielded by Weber Shandwick and by GJW's Adamson. As in the UK, the two are now one.

Clients may need help with legislation being drafted in the UK or abroad. European directives crafted in Brussels can bring an opportunity or a threat. Clients may find themselves having to defend or build their reputation before different audiences. Weber Shandwick | GJW claim to be the people to help, with experts specialising in government affairs, media relations, merger and acquisition, the planning process, healthcare and much else besides. They can also call upon the expertise of colleagues in the wider Weber Shandwick empire. They include the financial PR specialists at Square Mile, colleagues in corporate PR and in consumer PR, and their Change Marketing team who specialise in building staff morale by expert use of internal communications. Their senior staff have, variously, helped to create New Labour; worked for Tony Blair at Downing Street; served cabinet ministers during the Conservative party's long spell in power; occupied senior positions in the BBC and on broadsheet and tabloid newspapers.

They pride themselves on getting to understand their clients' needs - and on making sure senior executives are hands-on when dealing with the issues.

Background History

The public affairs practice of BSMG (Worldwide) was the UK's largest, incorporating Charles Barker Public Affairs, GJW Government Relations and LSA. Charles Barker was the UK's longest established public relations consultancy, having been founded in 1812 by Charles Barker himself. It introduced its public affairs service in 1969. In 1974 it merged with the oldest and best-known political consultancy, Watney & Powell and has clients dating back to the 1820s. In 1972 it became the first consultancy to offer specialised EEC services and in 1990 established its Brussels office. In the summer of 1997 it became part of the Bozell Sawyer Group of Communications companies which has a particularly strong public affairs lobbying and issues management operation in Washington.

In 1998 its parent company, BSMG Worldwide, acquired Brussels based public affairs company Adamson Associates. This then assumed responsibility for Charles Barker Public Affairs, Brussels. LSA joined BSMG in 1999. Then, in 2000, BSMG purchased GJW Government Relations, the UK's leading independent public affairs consultancy. GJW was founded in 1980 by Andrew Gifford (formerly assistant to Sir David Steel); the late Jenny Jeger (formerly assistant to Lord Callaghan) and Wilf Weeks (formerly assistant to Sir Edward Heath). Within months GJW had established itself as the model for modern practical consultancy and has been imitated ever since. In 1987 it sold out to Lowe Howard Spink and Bell for an estimated £5m. The company was bought back by its management in 1993.

In July 2001 True North, the Parent Company of BSMG, was purchased by The Interpublic Group which owns Weber Shandwick.

Westminster Strategy

Address	1 Deans Yard
	Westminster
	London
	SW1P 3NP
Telephone	020 7799 9811
Fax	020 7976 8276
E-mail	info@weststrat.co.uk
Website	www.westminsterstrategy.co.uk
Staff	25
Chairman	Michael Burrell
Chief Operating Officer	Susan Eastoe
Finance Director	David Attenbury Thomas
Directors	Jane Cooper, Paul Hannon
	Robbie MacDuff, Hugh Roberts
	David Robertson
Account Directors	Nicky Hughes, Dave Roberts
	Tony Sophoclides
Senior Account Managers	John Lehal, Tim Wilson
Account Managers	Karen Bermingham, Kate Wynne
Senior Account Executives	Cheryl Foreman, Chris Morritt
	Elizabeth Barlow, Richard Cox
	Tracey Crouch,
Account Executives	Cheryl Foreman, Chris Mornet
	Agnes Wheatcroft, Kevin Hoctor
	Rachel Lee
Year of Formation	1986
Estimated Fee Income	£2.5m
Parent Company	Grayling Group (Part of Havas Advertising)
Subsidiary Companies	Strategy in Scotland; Strategy Wales;
Associated Companies	Stormont Strategy (non-exclusive)
Brussels Office or Affiliate	Grayling Political Strategy
Trade Body Membership	APPC; PRCA; some staff are members of the NUJ
Code of Conduct	APPC

'Westminster Strategy have led the way in calls for statutory regulation of the public affairs industry. We pride ourselves on "know-how", not "know-who", and have an unparalleled reputation in upholding and promoting ethical standards. Grayling Political Strategy are leading members of the Association of Professional Political Consultants, whose code of conduct is based on our own company code. Our commitment to maintaining the highest professional standards, both in the service we offer to our clients and in our dealings with official institutions, is absolute.'

Company Information

Westminster Strategy is part of the Grayling Group, one of Europe's largest PR and public affairs consultancies. It is the London Headquarters of Grayling Political Strategy, with a total staff of thirty-two consultants. Grayling Political Strategy also incorporates Strategy in Scotland and Strategy Wales.

Westminster Strategy offer to help understand the political process, who the key players are, pinpoint where any potential challenges may lie and how best to influence those who matter in an honest and persuasive way.

Few clients have the same problems or priorities, so they customise their services to meet the client's needs. It may be that a simple political monitoring and intelligence service is required. At the other end of the spectrum, the client may be facing a severe threat to their core business which requires a comprehensive political and media relations programme.

Westminster Strategy offer:

*   research on, and analysis of, the relevant political issues of the day
*   early warning of forthcoming legislation and major policy initiatives
*   carefully researched identification of key decision makers and policy influencers
*   advice and assistance on the content and presentation of a client's case
*   strategic advice on the most effective means of approaching decision-makers
*   help in creating strategic alliances and working with third parties
*   preparation for Select Committee appearances
*   support for political briefing and contact activities

Formed in 1986, Westminster strategy was acquired by Lopex in 1988, which was subsequently acquired by Havas Advertising in 2000.

Winckworth Sherwood

Address

36 Great Peter Street
Westminster
London
SW1P 3LR

Partners and Parliamentary Agents	Alison Gorlov
	Paul Irving
	Christopher Vine
	Stephen Wiggs

Telephone	020 7593 5000
Fax	020 7593 5099
E-mail	info@winckworths.co.uk
Website	www.winckworths.co.uk

Company Information

Winckworth Sherwood is a firm of solicitors and parliamentary agents based in Westminster with offices in the City of London, Oxford and Chelmsford. They act for a wide range of clients drafting primary and secondary legislation, promoting bills in Parliament, managing Order applications and advising on practice and procedure.

Key areas include: Legislative procedures: Bills and Orders in Parliament; Transport and Works Orders; Harbour Orders; Scottish Provisional Orders and Private Bills; drafting constitutions, regulatory codes and other documents; byelaws.

Safeguarding interests: Amendments to public legislation; monitoring of parliamentary proceedings and research; objections and oppositions; nuisance claims.

2 **EU Lobbying Directory**

2M Public Affairs

Contact Name	Michel Maroy
Address	Square Vergote 39,
	B 1030 Brussels, Belgium
Telephone	0032 2 742 9456
Fax	0032 2 732 2251
E-mail	michael.maroy@skynet.be

Alva.com

Contact Name	Patrick Alvarez
Address	Rue des Tongres 24,
	B 1040 Brussels, Belgium
Telephone	0033 1 47645040
Fax	0033 1 40540216
E-mail	alvacom@wanadoo.fr
Website	www.alvacom

Anna MacDougald EU Public Affairs

UK Affilitate	Campaign Information Ltd
Address	Rue Louis Hap 195,
	1040 Brussels, Belgium
Telephone	0032 2 733 8785
Fax	0032 2 733 9255
E-mail	ameuconsult@compuserve.com

Anthonissen and Associates

Contact Name	Peter Frans Anthonissen
Address	Rue des Deux Eglises 37 Box 2,
	B 1000 Brussels, Belgium
Telephone	0032 2 230 5260
Fax	0032 2 230 5420

E-mail	anthonissen.associates@anthonissen.be
Website	www.anthonissen.be

APCO Europe

Contact Name	Bradley Staples
Address	Rue du Trone 130,
	B 1050 Brussels, Belgium
Telephone	0032 2 645 9811
Fax	0032 2 645 9812
E-mail	mail@apco-europe.com
Website	www.apcoassoc.com

Aran European Public Affairs

Contact Name	Deirdre Deady
Address	Av des Arts 24 box 8,
	B 1000 Brussels, Belgium
Telephone	0032 2 230 4763
Fax	0032 2 231 1772
E-mail	aranepa@skynet.be

Archimede

Contact Name	Richard Steel
Address	Rue Joseph II 36,
	B 1000 Brussels, Belgium
Telephone	0032 2 217 3939
Fax	0032 2 219 1842
E-mail	richard.steel@euronet.be

Atlantide Euro Service

Contact Name	Fiorenzo Grollino
Address	Av Louise 479,
	B 1050 Brussels, Belgium
Telephone	0032 2 646 5800
Fax	0032 2 646 7879
E-mail	aes@infoboard.be

Barabino & Partners Europe

Contact Name	Frederico Steiner
Address	Rue Theresienne 7,
	B 1000 Brussels, Belgium
Telephone	0032 2 502 1558

Fax	0032 2 502 4869
E-mail	f.stiner@barabino.be
Website	www.barabinoeurope.com

Bates and Wacker

Contact Name	Philippe Wacker
Address	Rue du Moniteur 9,
	B 1000 Brussels, Belgium
Telephone	0032 2 219 0305
Fax	0032 2 219 3215
E-mail	bw@eunet.be

BCP & Asociados Euroconsultores

Contact Name	Jesus Bores Lazo
Address	Rue Breydel 40A,
	B 1040 Brussels, Belgium
Telephone	0032 2 280 0125
Fax	0032 2 280 0130
E-mail	bcp@skynet.be
Website	www.bcp-asesores.com

Berenschot Belgium

Contact Name	Frank Vandewalle
Address	Av Marcel Thiry 81,
	B 1200 Brussels, Belgium
Telephone	0032 2 777 0645
Fax	0032 2 777 0646
E-mail	eurogmt@berenschot.com
Website	www.berenschot.com

Bircham Dyson Bell

UK Affilitate	Bircham Dyson Bell
Address	Rond Point Schuman 6, Box 5,
	B-1040 Brussels, Belguim
Telephone	0032 2 234 6306
Fax	0032 2 234 7911
E-mail	ppl@bdb-law.co.uk

BKSH Government Relations Worldwide

| Contact Name | Jeremy Galbraith |
| Address | Av de Cortenbergh 118, |

	B 1000 Brussels, Belgium
Telephone	0032 2 743 6666
Fax	0032 2 733 6611
E-mail	jeremy_galbraith@be.bm.com

Brussels Porter Novelli

Contact Name	Luc Missinne
Address	Bd Louis Mettewie 272,
	B 1050 Brussels, Belgium
Telephone	0032 2 413 0340
Fax	0032 2 413 0349
E-mail	luc.missinne@pnbrussels.com
Website	www.countrywidepn.co.uk

Burson-Marsteller

UK Affilitate	Burson-Marsteller/BKSH
Address	118 Avenue de Cortenbergh,
	B-1000 Brussels, Belgium
Telephone	0032 2 743 6611
Fax	0032 2 733 6611
E-mail	bm_brussels@eu.bm.com
Website	www.bmbrussels.be

Business Environment Europe

Contact Name	Bruno Liebhaberg
Address	Rue de Tacitume 42,
	B 1000 Brussels, Belgium
Telephone	0032 2 230 8360
Fax	0032 2 230 8370
E-mail	liebhaberg@bee.be

BW & Partners

Contact Name	Philippe Wacker
Address	Rue de Moniteur 9,
	B 1000 Brussels, Belgium
Telephone	0032 2 219 0305
Fax	0032 2 219 3215
E-mail	bwp@planetinternet.be

Cabinet Stewart

Contact Name	Catherine Steward
Address	Rue d'Arlon 40,
	B 1000 Brussels, Belgium
Telephone	0032 2 230 7020
Fax	0032 2 5043
E-mail	cabinetstewart@cabinetstewart.com

CB Europa

Contact Name	Ignacio Corrochano
Address	Av. d'Auderghem 76,
	B 1040 Brussels, Belgium
Telephone	0032 2 732 3333
Fax	0032 2 732 8990
E-mail	info@cbeuropa.com
Website	www.cbeuropa.com

Citigate Public Affairs

Contact Name	Thierry Lebeaux
Address	Av de Cortenbergh 66,
	B 1000 Brussels, Belgium
Telephone	0032 2 736 8135
Fax	0032 2 736 8847
E-mail	thierry.lebeaux@citigate.co.uk
Website	www.incepta.co.uk

Clan Public Affairs

Contact Name	Daniel Gueguen
Address	Rue Froissart 57-59,
	B 1040 Brussels, Belgium
Telephone	0032 2 736 5800
Fax	0032 2 738 7120
E-mail	clanpa@clan-public-affairs.be
Website	www.clan-public-affairs.be

Communications Group

Contact Name	Terry Davidson
Address	Av Louise 497,
	B 1050 Brussels, Belgium
Telephone	0032 2 640 9207
Fax	0032 2 640 9224

E-mail	terry@eurocom.be
Website	www.eurocom.be

Conseille
Contact Name	Silvana Koch-Mehrin
Address	Chee de Wavre 214C,
	B 1050 Brussels, Belgium
Telephone	0032 2 230 8575
Fax	0032 2 231 0601
E-mail	fsh@conseille.com
Website	www.conseille.com

CPS
Contact Name	Tulu Gumustekin
Address	Av des Arts 27,
	B 1040 Brussels, Belgium
Telephone	0032 2 237 9940
Fax	0032 2 237 9960
E-mail	tulu.gumustekin@cpsag.com
Website	www.cpsag.com

Decitime
Contact Name	Evelyn Gessler
Address	Chee de Charleroi 96,
	B 1060 Brussels, Belgium
Telephone	0032 2 534 6686
Fax	0032 2 534 6698
E-mail	decitime@decitime.be
Website	www.decitime.be

J.M. Didier & Associates European Affairs
Contact Name	JM Didier
Address	Rue Vergote 11,
	B 1030 Brussels, Belgium
Telephone	0032 2 736 9910
Fax	0032 2 736 8994
E-mail	didierassociates@compuserve.com

DLA Upstream
UK Affilitate	DLA Upstream
Address	106 Avenue Louise,

	B-1050 Brussels, Belgium
Telephone	0032 2 629 6969
Fax	0032 2 629 6970
E-mail	kajsa.stenstroem@dla.com
Website	www.dla-upstream.com

Eamonn Bates European Public Affairs

Contact Name	Eamonn Bates
Address	Av d'Auderghem 67,
	B 1040 Brussels, Belgium
Telephone	0032 2 286 9494
Fax	0032 2 286 9495
E-mail	info@eamonnbates.com

Ecotec Research & Counsulting

Contact Name	Adrian Healy
Address	Av de Tervuren 13B,
	B 1040 Brussels, Belgium
Telephone	0032 2 743 8922
Fax	0032 2 732 7111
E-mail	adrian_healy@ecotec.com
Website	www.ecotec.com

Edelman Europe

UK Affilitate	Edelman UK
Address	20 Rue des Deux Eglises,
	B-1000 Brussels, Belguim
Telephone	0032 2 227 6170
Fax	0032 2 227 6189
E-mail	request@edelman.com
Website	www.edelman.com

Entente International Communication SA

UK Affilitate	The Communication Group
Address	7 Rue Theresienne,
	B-1000 Brussels, Belguim
Telephone	0032 2 502 1558
Fax	0032 2 502 4869
E-mail	political@thecommunicationgroup.co.uk

Environmental Policy Centre Europe

Contact Name	T. Dumortier
Address	Rue de Mail 13-15,
	B 1050 Brussels, Belgium
Telephone	0032 2 775 9797
Fax	0032 2 775 9799
E-mail	epce@epce.com
Website	www.epce.com

Environmental Resources Management

Contact Name	Walter Buydens
Address	Rue des Poissonnieres 13,
	B 1000 Brussels, Belgium
Telephone	0032 2 550 0280
Fax	0032 2 550 0299
E-mail	sd@ermbelgium.be
Website	www.erm.com

Epsilon

Contact Name	Henning Chirstophersen
Address	Rue de Toulouse 49,
	B 1040 Brussels, Belgium
Telephone	0032 2 230 0081
Fax	0032 2 230 1086
E-mail	epsilon@epsilon-consulting.be

Essor Europe

Contact Name	Phillippe de Montgolfier
Address	Rue de Treves 45,
	B 1040 Brussels, Belgium
Telephone	0032 2 230 2294
Fax	0032 2 231 0838
E-mail	mailbox@essoreurope.fr
Website	www.essoreurope.fr

EU.Select

Contact Name	Werner Bohrer
Address	Rue du Commerce 31,
	B 1000 Brussels, Belguim
Telephone	0032 2 548 9010
Fax	0032 2 548 9019.

E-mail   info@eu-select.com
Website   www.eu-select.com

Euralia Group

UK Affilitate   Keene Public Affairs Consultants
Contact Name   Bruno Dupont
Address   Rue Montoyer 47,
                                       B-1000 Brussels, Belgium
Telephone   0032 2 506 8820
Fax   0032 2 506 8825
E-mail   info@euralia.com
Website   www.euralia.com

Euroc

Contact Name   A David
Address   Av A Huysmans 74,
                                       B 1050 Brussels, Belgium
Telephone   0032 2 675 3326
Fax   0032 2 779 9563
E-mail   euroc_be@yahoo.com

Europe Analytica

Contact Name   Douglas Herbison
Address   Avenue Livingstone 25 (Bte 3),
                                       B 1000 Brussels, Belguim
Telephone   0032 2 231 1299
Fax   0032 2 230 7658
E-mail   info@europe-analytica.com
Website   www.european-analytica.com

European Advisory Services

Contact Name   Simon Pettman
Address   Rue de l'Association 50,
                                       B 1000 Brussels, Belgium
Telephone   0032 2 218 1470
Fax   0032 2 219 7342
E-mail   info@eas.be
Website   www.eas.be

European Consulting Company

Contact Name	Jonathan Bott
Address	Av des Gaulois 9,
	B 1040 Brussels, Belgium
Telephone	0032 2 736 5354
Fax	0032 2 732 3427
E-mail	euroconsult@ecco.be
Website	www.ecco.be

European Contact Service

Contact Name	Eric Damiens
Address	Av A Lacomble 66,
	B 1030 Brussels, Belgium
Telephone	0032 2 737 7742
Fax	0032 2 732 6608
E-mail	ecos@eis.be
Website	www.eis.be

European Expert Institute

Contact Name	Marc Clerens
Address	Square Vergote 39,
	B 1030 Brussels, Belgium
Telephone	0032 2 743 2900
Fax	0032 2 743 2990
E-mail	eeim@eei.be

European Policy and Communications Advisory Services

Contact Name	Alessandro Profili
Address	Av Marquis de Villalobar 88,
	B 1150 Brussels, Belgium
Telephone	0032 2 762 5661
Fax	0032 2 762 5317
E-mail	aprofili@skynet.be

European Project

Contact Name	Giulio Ripa di Meana
Address	Av Mamix 19A,
	B 1000 Brussels, Belgium
Telephone	0032 2 512 7980
Fax	0032 2 514 2119
E-mail	epro@online.be

European Public Policy Advisers

Contact Name	Pascal Michaux
Address	Palace du Luxembourg 2,
	B 1050 Brussels, Belgium
Telephone	0032 2 735 8230
Fax	0032 2 735 4412
E-mail	julius.waller@eppa.com
Website	www.eppa.com

European Strategy and Lobbying

Contact Name	Simon Wreford-Howard
Address	Rue de la Loi 81 A,
	B 1040 Brussels, Belgium
Telephone	0032 2 230 5629
Fax	0032 2 230 5319
E-mail	annabellet@esinetwork.com

Eurotec Consulting

Contact Name	Alberto D'Alessandro
Address	Rond-Point Schuman 9 box 15,
	B 1040 Brussels, Belgium
Telephone	0032 2 282 0080
Fax	0032 2 230 3168
E-mail	info@eurotec.be
Website	www.eurotec.be

Eurowin Communications

Contact Name	Marc Callemien
Address	Av de la Fontaine 31,
	B 1435 Brussels, Belgium
Telephone	0032 10 658 903
Fax	0032 10 658448
E-mail	marc.callemien@euronet.be

FIPRA EU

Contact Name	Peter-Carlo Lehrell
Address	Bd St-Michel 47,
	B 1040 Brussels, Belgium
Telephone	0032 2 737 7632
Fax	0032 2 737 7698
E-mail	enquiries@fipra.com
Website	www.fipra.com

GBAT Beckenham

Contact Name	Graham Austin
Address	Rue des Compagnons 50 box 2,
	B 1030 Brussels, Belgium
Telephone	0032 2 726 1579
Fax	0032 2 726 1759
E-mail	gbat.beckenham@skynet.be

GCI Brussels

Contact Name	Simon Titley
Address	Db de la Woluwe 56 box 5,
	B 1200 Brussels, Belgium
Telephone	0032 2 776 7830
Fax	0032 2 776 7839
E-mail	stitley@gcibrussels.com
Website	www.gcigroup.com

Gellis Communications SPRL

UK Affilitate	August.One Public Affairs
Address	Rue des Echevins 80,
	B-1050 Brussels, Belgium
Telephone	0032 2 347 3482
Fax	0032 2 347 0024
E-mail	gellis@skynet.be

Global Europe

Contact Name	Daniel Villaneuve
Address	Av Louise 179,
	B 1050 Brussels, Belgium
Telephone	0032 2 640 1259
Fax	0032 2 647 7328
E-mail	global.europe@global-eu.com
Website	www.global-eu.com

GPC International

Contact Name	Caroline Wunnerlich
Address	Rue d'Arlon 50,
	B-1000 Brussels, Belgium
Telephone	0032 2 230 0545
Fax	0032 2 230 5706
E-mail	caroline.wunnerlich@gpcbrussels.com
Website	www.gpcinternational.com

Grayling Political Strategy

UK Affilitates	Grayling Political Strategy: Westminster Strategy; Strategy in Scotland; Strategy Wales; Stormont Strategy
Address	58 Avenue des Arts, B-1000 Brussels, Belgium
Telephone	0032 2 732 7040
Fax	0032 2 732 71776
E-mail	info@grayling-ps.com
Website	www.grayling-ps.com

Hall Aitken Associates

Contact Name	Peter Hall
Address	Rue Belliard 205 box 3, B 1040 Brussels, Belgium
Telephone	0032 2 230 0918
Fax	0032 2 231 1262
E-mail	hall.aitken@chello.be
Website	www.hallaitken.co.uk

Heidi Lambert Communications

Contact Name	Heidi Lambert
Address	Rue Stevin 212, B 1000 Brussels, Belgium
Telephone	0032 2 732 5546
Fax	0032 2 735 3603
E-mail	hlc@skynet.be

Hill and Knowlton Int. Belgium

UK Affilitate	Hill and Knowlton UK
Address	Avenue de Cortenbergh 118, B-1000 Brussels, Belgium
Telephone	0032 2 737 9500
Fax	0032 2 737 9501
E-mail	ecruiksh@hillandknowlton.com
Website	www.hillandknowlton.be

Houston Consulting Europe

Contact Name	John Houston
Address	Av de la Joyeuse Entrée 1-5, B 1000 Brussels, Belgium

Telephone	0032 2 504 8040
Fax	0032 2 504 8050
E-mail	info@houston-consulting.com
Website	www.houston-consulting.com

IBF International Consulting

Contact Name	Frederic Andre
Address	Rue Montoyer 63,
	B 1000 Brussels, Belgium
Telephone	0032 2 237 0906
Fax	0032 2 230 4649
E-mail	ibf@ibf.be

ICODA

Contact Name	Dr. Lodewijk Buschkens
Address	Rue de Sceptre 63A,
	B 1050 Brussels, Belgium
Telephone	0032 2 649 7495
Fax	0032 2 649 1341
E-mail	ahem@icoda.com
Website	www.icoda.com

Interel European Public Affairs

Contact Name	Fredrik Lofthagen
Address	Av de Tervuren 402,
	B 1150 Brussels, Belguim
Telephone	0032 2 761 6611
Fax	0032 2 777 0504
E-mail	epa@intermar.be
Website	www.intermar.be/iepa

Interel Marien

Contact Name	Jean-Leopold Schuybroek
Address	Av de Tervuren 402,
	B 1150 Brussels, Belgium
Telephone	0032 2 761 6611
Fax	0032 2 761 6600
E-mail	info@intermar.be
Website	www.intermar.be

International Relations Consulting

Contact Name	Peter Bahr
Address	Av. Louise 225 box 9,
	B 1050 Brussels, Belgium
Telephone	0032 2 640 1869
Fax	0032 2 648 2161
E-mail	general@ireico.com
Website	www.ireico.com

International Technology and Trade Associates

Contact Name	Ronald E Baker
Address	Av. Louise 65 box 11,
	B 1050 Brussels, Belgium
Telephone	0032 2 535 7898
Fax	0032 2 535 7700
E-mail	bakermrc@compuserve.com
Website	www.itta.com

IP Strategies

Contact Name	Louis Veyret
Address	Chee de Louvain 490,
	B 1380 Brussels, Belgium
Telephone	0032 2 351 0011
Fax	0032 2 351 0114
E-mail	info@ipstrategies.com
Website	www.ipstrategies.com

Kate Thomas & Kleyn

Contact Name	Kaat L Exterbille
Address	Av Baron de Viron 5,
	B 1700 Brussels, Belgium
Telephone	0032 2 569 3644
Fax	0032 2 569 7480
E-mail	info@kate.thomas.kleyn.be
Website	www.katethomaskleyn.be

Kreab Brussels

Contact Name	Georg Danell
Address	Av de Tervuren 13A,
	B 1040 Brussels, Belgium
Telephone	0032 2 737 6900

Fax	0032 2 737 6940
E-mail	kreab@kreab.com

L Consult - European Affairs

Contact Name	Marie-Christine Lefebvre
Address	Square Marie-Louise 40 box 31,
	B 1000 Brussels, Belgium
Telephone	0032 2 230 1390
Fax	0032 2 230 1737
E-mail	lconsult@unicall.be

Latimer Europa

Contact Name	Paolo Celot
Address	Roind-Point Schuman 9 Box 16,
	B 1040 Brussels, Belguim
Telephone	0032 2 282 0084
Fax	0032 2 230 3006
E-mail	celot@latimer.com

Lobbycom

Contact Name	Jean-Marie de Vliegher
Address	Dieweg 252,
	B 1180 Brussels, Belgium
Telephone	0032 2 372 0093
Fax	0032 2 534 7231
E-mail	lobby@skynet.be
Website	www.lobbycom.com

Logos European Affairs

Contact Name	Jose Lalloum
Address	Rue Vautier 54,
	B 1050 Brussels, Belgium
Telephone	0032 2 639 6230
Fax	0032 2 644 9017
E-mail	secretariat@logos-eu.com

Metzdorff & Associates

Contact Name	Carl Metzdorff
Address	Av de la Ferme Rose 9A
	box 21,
	B 1180 Brussels, Belgium

Telephone	0032 2 346 1699
Fax	0032 2 346 1699
E-mail	c.metzdorff@aces.be

MVV Consultants and Engineers

Contact Name	Jorg Matthies
Address	Av Jules Cesar 9,
	B 1150 Brussels, Belgium
Telephone	0032 2 763 2128
Fax	0032 2 770 1041
E-mail	brussels@consultants.mvv.de
Website	www.consultants.mvv.de

Nicholas Phillips Associates

Contact Name	Nicholas Phillips
Address	Rue Joseph II 36 box 9,
	B 1000 Brussels, Belgium
Telephone	0032 2 218 1370
Fax	0032 2 219 1842
E-mail	nicholas.phillips@euronet.be

One Market

Contact Name	Pal Jacobsen
Address	Rue de la Tourelle 37,
	B 1040 Brussels, Belgium
Telephone	0032 2 231 1884
Fax	0032 2 280 0690
E-mail	one.market@pophost.eunet.be
Website	www.one-market.org

P & A Consultores

Contact Name	Enrique Bercero Aguado
Address	Square Marie-Louise 1,
	B 1000 Brussels, Belgium
Telephone	0032 2 282 3782
Fax	0032 2 282 3783
E-mail	bruselas@pyaconsultores.com
Website	www.pyaconsultores.com

Pantheion

Contact Name	Peter Theunisz
Address	Rue des Deux Eglises 124,
	B 1210 Brussels, Belgium
Telephone	0032 2 280 6100
Fax	0032 2 280 6100
E-mail	info@pantheion.com
Website	www.pantheion.com

Pathfinders

Contact Name	Marie-Christine Ashby
Address	Dreve de Richelle 104,
	B 1410 Waterloo, Belgium
Telephone	0032 2 351 0073
Fax	0032 2 351 0073
E-mail	pathfinders@freegates.be

PLS Ramboll Management

Contact Name	Leif Stoy
Address	Rue de Crayer 5,
	B 1000 Brussels, Belgium
Telephone	0032 2 649 9983
Fax	0032 2 649 0188
E-mail	pla@pls-ramboll.com
Website	www.pla-ramboll.com

Policy Options and Development Strategy

Contact Name	William Seddon-Brown
Address	Bd du Souverain 146,
	B 1160 Brussels, Belgium
Telephone	0032 2 660 8031
Fax	0032 2 660 7267
E-mail	seddon@optinet.be

Political Intelligence (Belgium)

UK Affilitate	Political Intelligence
Address	39 Rue Montoyer BP3,
	B-1000 Brussels, Belgium
Telephone	0032 2 503 2265
Fax	0032 2 503 42 95
E-mail	info@political-intelligence.com
Website	www.political-intelligence.com

Praaning Meines Consultancy

Contact Name	Rio D Praaning
Address	Rue Franklin 108,
	B 1000 Brussels, Belgium
Telephone	0032 2 735 8396
Fax	0032 2 735 8466
E-mail	info@praaningmeines.be

PricewaterhouseCoopers

Address	Avenue de Cortenbergh 75,
	B-1000 Brussels, Belgium
Telephone	0032 2 741 0811
Fax	0032 2 741 0892
E-mail	davies.mike@be.pwcglobal.com
Website	www.pwcglobal.com/epa

Prisma Consulting Group (The)

Contact Name	Peter Wilmott
Address	Rue de Luxembourg 3,
	B 1000 Brussels, Belgium
Telephone	0032 2 501 0820
Fax	0032 2 501 0830
E-mail	info@prismaconsulting.com
Website	www.prismaconsulting.com

PRM European Lobbyists

UK Affilitate	Politics International Ltd.
Address	10 Rue Berckmans,
	B-1060 Brussels, Belgium
Telephone	0032 2 649 3533
Fax	0032 2 649 2593
E-mail	prm@prmltd.com
Website	www.prismaconsulting.com

Promar Ceas International

Contact Name	Conrad Caspari
Address	Av E Plasky 22,
	B 1030 Brussels, Belgium
Telephone	0032 2 736 0088
Fax	0032 2 732 1361
E-mail	info@promar-ceas.com
Website	www.promar-international.com

PRP

UK Affilitate	Golin/Harris Ludgate
Address	5 The Avenue,
	Rue Vandendriessche,
	B-1150 Brussels, Belgium
Telephone	0032 2 762 0485
Fax	0032 2 771 1959
E-mail	info@prp.be

Puyenbroek Intelligence Access

Contact Name	Maninus Puyenbroek
Address	Hammeveld 6,
	B 3061 Brussels, Belgium
Telephone	0032 2 767 0790
Fax	0032 2 768 0269
E-mail	marinus.puyenbroek@worldonline.be

Robin Linton Associates

Address	Av de Cortenbergh,
	B 1000 Brussels, Belgium
Telephone	0032 2 743 6666
Fax	0032 2 733 6611

The Rowland Company

Contact Name	Abigail Jones
Address	Imperiastraast 16,
	B 1930 Brussels, Belgium
Telephone	0032 2 512 0919
Fax	0032 2 512 4120
Website	www.roland.com

Saces

Contact Name	Mario Corvey
Address	Rue de la Concorde 19-20,
	B 1050 Brussels, Belgium
Telephone	0032 2 511 8120
Fax	0032 2 511 9943
E-mail	saces@saces.com

Schuman Associates

Contact Name	Gerard Macnamara
Address	Rue Archimede 5,
	B 1000 Brussels, Belgium
Telephone	0032 2 230 7439
Fax	0032 2 230 7426
E-mail	info@schumanassociates.com
Website	www.schumanassociates.com

SDD Petosevic

Contact Name	Slobodan Petosevic
Address	Hyelaan 6,
	B 3090 Brussels, Belgium
Telephone	0032 2 688 3315
Fax	0032 2 688 3316
E-mail	mail@petosevic.com
Website	www.petosevic.com

Shandwick Public Affairs

Contact Name	John Russell
Address	Av de Tervuren 12 box 11,
	B 1040 Brussels, Belgium
Telephone	0032 2 743 4220
Fax	0032 2 743 4222
E-mail	spabrussels@shandwick.com
Website	www.shandwick.com

Strategies and Communications

Contact Name	Luc Domoulin
Address	Av des Phalenes 26,
	B 1000 Brussels, Belgium
Telephone	0032 2 649 6282
Fax	0032 2 649 1885
E-mail	info@stratcom.be
Website	www.stratcom.be

The Waterfront Partnership

UK Affilitate	The Waterfront Partnership
Address	London House, Rue Breydel 40,
	B 1040 Brussels, Belgium
Telephone	0032 2 282 9515

Weber Shandwick Public Affairs

Address	Avenue de Tervuren, 12 bte 11,
	B-1040 Brussels, Belgium
Telephone	0032 2 743 4220
Fax	0032 2 743 4222

Westminster Europe

Contact Name	Greg Perry
Address	Av de Cortenbergh 66,
	B 1000 Brussels, Belgium
Telephone	0032 2 736 8135
Fax	0032 2 736 8847

Wissenraet & Van Spaendonck Ass. Management

Contact Name	Ullrich Schroder
Address	Av de la Joyeuse Entrée 1,
	B 1040 Brussels, Belgium
Telephone	0032 2 285 0020
Fax	0032 2 285 0024
E-mail	vsw@spaendonck.nl

Worldcom Europe Brussels

Contact Name	Stefan Chrobok
Address	Rue Belliard 159,
	B 1040 Brussels, Belgium
Telephone	0032 2 280 6061
Fax	0032 2 280 6059
E-mail	w.e.b@skynet.com

Zenab

Contact Name	Nicole La Bouverie
Address	Av Beau-Sejour 46,
	B 1180 Brussels, Belgium
Telephone	0032 2 640 0034
Fax	0032 2 640 0241
E-mail	zenab@skynet.com

3 Who's Who in Lobbying

Adams, Mark OBE

Managing Director, Foresight Communications

Graduate of Cambridge University (Economics), MSc. Economics and Econometrics. From June 1984 until December 1991, worked at the Department of Employment, representing Government policy to external bodies including at the European Union. From January 1992 until December 1997 he worked at the heart of Government working as Private Secretary to two Prime Ministers, John Major and Tony Blair, advising on all parliamentary matters and preparation for Prime Minister's Questions. Since then, worked as a Director at two consultancies, including APCO, before founding Foresight Communications in January 2001.

Adamson, Paul

CEO, Adamson BSMG Worldwide

In 1979, worked as a research aide to two British members of the European Parliament before becoming the first British graduate to enrol in the newly-created European University Institute in Florence, where he studied European politics for three years. He recently completed a three-year term as Chairman of the EU Committee of the British Chamber of Commerce in Brussels and has served on the Executive Commitee and Policy Group of the American Chamber of Commerce's EU Committee. He sold his company, Adamson Associates, to BSMG in 1998 and is CEO of Adamson BSMG Worldwide and head of BSMG European Public Affairs.

Aitken, Carol

Managing Director, APCO Scotland

Graduate of Stirling University (French and Philosophy). Joined the Lord Chancellor's Department and in 1992 went to work in the House of Commons for a Conservative MP. In 1997 she joined the Chemical Industries Association in 1997, monitoring and lobbying the European Parliament and developing resonponses to the Scottish Parliament.

Anderson, Iain

Executive Director & Chief Corporate Counsel, Cicero Consulting

Graduate of St. Andrews University (MA in Politics, Management and Economics), University of Wales (Postgraduate Diploma in Journalism). House of Commons researcher for Conservative MP, Henry Bellingham, who was then PPS to the Secretary of State for Transport, Malcolm Rifkind. In 1991 he studied and gained a post-graduate diploma in journalism and then covered the 1992 General Election for the Glasgow Herald.

Became a journalist on the financial trade publication *Money Marketing* before becoming a founding shareholder and journalist on *Investment Week* in 1994. Joined Ludgate Communications in 1997, where he was appointed a divisional director of Ludgate Public Affairs. Left in 2000 to co-found Cicero Consulting.

Arnold, John

Director, PoliticsDirect

President of Stirling University where he gained a degree in Business Studies and Economics. Then became Chair of Scottish Labour Students before being appointed Adviser to the Shadow Secretary of State for Scotland. Joined the Local Government International Bureau where he became Head of the International Section. Moved to The Communication Group plc, London, as a Senior Consultant before becoming Divisional Board Director and then acting Managing Director of the political division. In September 1999, he became a founding Director of PoliticsDirect.com.

Ashton, Terry

Consultant, Butler Kelly

Former General Secretary of the Greater London Labour Party, managing the Party in London for over 12 years; involved in selection process for Lonson MPs, MEPs and GLA members, political liaison with Labour's London Parliamentary Group with local authorities.

Atack, Steve

Editor and Publisher, Public Affairs Newsletter

Eastbourne College of Education, President of Student Union 1972/73. Former Councillor and Parliamentary Candidate. National Chairman of the Young Liberal Movement, 1975-76. Publisher of the Public Affairs Newsletter and proprietor of Public Affairs Executive Search Consultancy. Encyclopedic knowledge of the public affairs industry and its actors.

Awford, Suzy

Senior Policy and Information Executive, DLA Upstream

Former civil servant at the Department of the Clerk at the House of Commons. Head of Research and European Affairs Team Manager at A S Biss.

Barlow, Harry

Managing Director, Harry Barlow Ltd.

Graduate of the London School of Economics (BSc, PhD). 1984-86 Head of Publicity, Greater London Council. Director of Issue Communications from 1984-1999, clients included the Norwegian Government, the League against Cruel Sports and the National Environmental Protection Board - Sweden. Director of Harry Barlow Ltd., including responsibilities such as Communications Adviser to the Mayor of London. Fellow of the Royal Geographic Society. Member of the Institute of Public Relations and committee member of the LSE London Committee.

Barnes, Paul

Senior Director, Weber Shandwick | GJW

Graduate in Politics and Economics. Ran the public relations section of his family business whilst being a member of North Norfolk District Council for 8 years. Secretary of the Council's Conservative Group, and at 23, became Britain's youngest Mayor. Joined GJW/BSMG in 1989. Chair of Governors of Hackney Community College.

Barwick, Steve

Director, Connect Public Affairs

Former senior adviser to Rt Hon Margaret Beckett MP, has also been a media relations adviser to Alice Mahon MP and Dawn Primarolo MP. Prior to the 97 election, played a key role in Labour Party policy formation on health. Has a number of years experience in local government, including being a Labour Councillor. Recently completed studies for a Masters in Politics and Administration from Birkbeck College.

Bas, Jenina

Managing Director, Tim Pendry - Public Affairs, Public Relations, Media Relations

Background in journalism, where she edited East Asia's second largest women's magazine. Moved into PR to manageone of the leading companies in Singapore, before moving to London when it was taken over. Creator of the ParentPower concept as a credible non-regulatory alternative to external regulation in the advertising industry.

Baverstock, Paul

Chief Operating Officer, Bell Pottinger

Graduate of Harvard University (BA Modern Political History), Yale University (MBA, School of Management). Strategic management consultant with A T Kearney and Mitchell Madison Group before becoming Chief Executive of LLM. Joined Bell Pottinger in October 1999, where he became Managing Director. In 2001 moved to become Chief Operating Officer of the Bell Pottinger group of compaines and joined the board of Bell Pottinger Consultants.

Bearman, Kate

Director, Lexington Communications

Formerly a Senior Consultant with GPC Market Access.

Beamer, David

Director, PoliticsDirect

Graduate of Aston University (Business) and the University of Miami, Florida. In January 1995, he joined the Conservative Research Department as Desk Officer for Trade and Industry, and Transport. In 1996, he was made Head of Home Affairs and worked on the Health, National Heritage and Wales briefs. Then joined The Communication Group plc (TCG) in December 1997 as a consultant and was appointed Director of Healthcare in May 1999. He left TCG in September 1999 to become a founding Director of PoliticsDirect.com.

Bell, Kevin

Managing Director and Vice-Chairman, GPC London

Graduate of Reading University. Former adviser to Conservative candidates in the '79, '83, '87 and '92 General Elections. In the early 1980s he was a director of Michael Forsyth Associates before joining the Grayling Company in 1984. From 1986 to 1994 he was a Director of Westminster Strategy before joining Bell Pottinger as Managing Director. Now Managing Director of GPC London.

Bell, Tim (Lord)

Chairman, Bell Pottinger

Started with ABC TV in 1959 before joining Colman Prentis & Varley. Chairman and Managing Director of Saatchi for 10 years before becoming Group Chief Executive of Lowe Howard Spink in 1985. Former Director of the Centre for Policy Studies, also adviser to the NCB Chairman in the mid-eighties and a key adviser to the then Prime Minister, Margaret Thatcher.

Bennett, David

Director, Citigate Public Affairs

Graduate of the University of London (Economics) and Post-Graduate of Johns Hopkins University School of Advanced International Studies (International Relations). Started career working with the European Commission and subsequently became a public affairs adviser for the British Gas Corporation before moving into consultancy. Formerly Managing Director of Powerhouse Europe. Speaks regularly for the European Commission on internal market and EMU issues. Served as Chairman of the National Association of Mutual Guarantee Societies and as a Director of the European Association of Mutual Guarantee Schemes. A former Parliamentary Candidate (SDP/Alliance), and a European Parliamentary candidate. A Director of the APPC and a member of the IPR. Founded Beaumark in 1992, which was aquired by Citgate Public Affairs in 2001, where he took on the role of Director.

Bentham, Clara

Account Manager, LLM Communications

Formerly a Parliamentary Executive at the Parliamentary Information Unit. During the 1997 election she worked in Labour's Rapid Rebuttal Unit at Millbank Tower.

Bevington, Gill

Research and Translations Manager, Perchards

Worked for UNICEF in New York and West Africa and was research assistant to a number of MPs and MEPs before joining Perchards in 1991. Independent expert member of the Producer Responsibility Operators' Forum set up by the Department of the Environment, Transport and the Regions. Member of the Institute of Linguists.

Bigg, Alex

Account Director, Corporate and Public Affairs, Edelman London

Previously a Senior Consultant at Shandwick Public Affairs, joined Edelman in December 2000.

Biggar, Allan

President and CEO, Burson-Marsteller UK

Former Chief of Staff to Sir David Steel, Leader of the Liberal Democrats, advising senior politicians at the highest levels. Worked in the UK Parliament on issues related to the first UK privatisation legislation, the flotation of British Telecom and other utilities. Joined Burson-Marsteller and prior to 1997 was Managing Director of Burson-Marsteller Middle East and North Africa. Team leader of Burson-Marsteller's privatisation group in Egypt and established a public affairs unit for the Minister of Public Enterprise. From 1997-2000, based in Brussels he was European Public Affairs Practice Chair and Market Leader of the Burson-Marsteller Brussels office. In 2001, became Market Leader of the London office and President and CEO of Burson Marsteller UK.

Bingle, Peter

Managing Director, Bell Pottinger

Previously Managing Director of The Communications Group and GPC in London. Appointed Managing Director in 2001.

Biss, Adele

Founder, AS Biss

Prior to forming AS Biss in 1996, spent three years as Chairman of the British Tourist Authority and the English Tourist Board. Founder and Chief Executive of Biss Lancaster, and has been Non-Executive Director of Eurostar Ltd and of Harry Ramsden's, having served previously on the British Railway's Board for five years. She is a council member of the Girls Day School Trust and a governor of University College, London and Middlesex University where she also chairs the Ethics committee for the Chinese Traditional Medicine degree course.

Booth, John

Director and Non-executive Chairman, Luther Pendragon

Held this position since the company's inception in 1992. Has worked in finance since 1983 in a variety of roles, latterly as managing director of Bankers Trust's Global Equities business. Chairs four other companies in the Internet, telecoms and financial products sectors and is widely involved in venture capital and investment.

Bourne, Steve

Public Affairs Manager, The Waterfront Partnership

Between 1995 and 1998, worked in the Ministerial Private Office of the Department of Health, before joining the Waterfront Partnership in 1998.

Bowyer, Peter

Director, Weber Shandwick | GJW

Former lecturer in European Politics and Press and Policy Adviser to Tom Pendry MP, the former Shadow Sport and Tourism Minister and now Chairman of the Football Foundation. Joined BSMG in 1996 and advised on major government and media relations campaigns. Seconded to the Labour Party during the 1997 election campaign. Became BSMG Worldwide Associate Director in London before moving to join the board of Shandwick

Public Affairs as a Director. Has also been a press officer to a Labour controlled local government association and an assistant lecturer in two university politics departments.

Boyd, Jim

Director, Consolidated Communications

Graduate of Edinburgh University (Philosophy). Former International Tax Lawyer, and is founding Director of the flourishing Consolidated Communications' public affairs team. Advised Thames Trains during the Paddington Disaster, and was the unpaid campaign adviser to the Save Barts' Campaign. Stood as the Conservative Parliamentary Candidate for Sunderland South in the 2001 General Election, achieving a 2.7% swing from Labour. Vice-Chair of the Public Relations Consultants Association's Public Affairs Committee.

Bracken, Jonathan

Partner, Parliamentary and Public Law, Bircham Dyson Bell

Before entering private practice Jonathan was a regulatory lawyer in the Lloyd's insurance market and for more than a decade worked at the UK House of Commons as a researcher and policy adviser for a group of Conservative Members of Parliament. Joined Bircham Dyson Bell in 1991 and is a partner in the firm's specialist Parliamentary and Public Law practice. Currently scholar in residence at the United States Law Library of Congress and is joint editor (with Paul Thompson) of Parliaments and Assemblies of the United Kingdom.

Bramall, Stephen

Deputy Managing Director, The Waterfront Partnership

Former research assistant to Michael Portillo. From 1974-90, worked in the Department of Transport, holding a range of posts. Worked on four Transport Bills and between 1987-89 was the Principal Private Secretary to successive Ministers of State for Transport. Joined GJW in 1990 and moved to Market Access two years later to head their Transport Unit. Joined the Waterfront Partnership in 1996. Has served as a Director of the APPC.

Brice, Joe

Account Director, PR21

Graduate of Hull University (Politics and Legislative Studies). Research Assistant for Conservative MP Sebastian Coe OBE and co-ordinator for the Conservative West Country Members Group prior to joining PR21 in April 1996.

Bridges, George MBE

Quiller Consultants

Graduate of Exeter College, Oxford (Modern History). In 1991, was awarded a Thouron Scholarship to the Fels Centre of Government at the University of Pennsylvania. Joined Downing Street from the Conservative Research Department. There, he worked in the Economic Section during the 1992 General Election campaign, and then as an adviser to the Education Secretary. Spent three and a half years at 10 Downing Street, where he was Assistant Political Secretary to the Prime Minister. His main roles were writing speeches and articles for the Prime Minister, and preparing briefing for interviews and Parliamentary questions. Before joining Quiller Consultants, George spent almost two years as a leader writer at The Times, where he wrote editorials about domestic politics and social policy (including issues such as genetically modified foods, agriculture and education). He joined the newspaper after spending a year as Head of Communications for Britain's only commercial digital terrestrial television company, ONDigital.

Brown, Nicholas

Partner, Bircham Dyson Bell

Graduate of Jesus College, Oxford. Joined Bircham Dyson Bell in 1979 and became a partner and Roll 'A' Parliamentary Agent in 1985. Chariman of the firm's Executive Committee.

Brown, Tony

Executive Vice-President, Chelgate

Began career as full time researcher to Lynda Chalker, then Shadow Junior Minister for the DHSS. Also worked for Stephen Dorrell MP. Over 20 years PR experience, particularly in the fields of environment, transport, health and defence. The 1997 Conservative Parliamentary Candidate for Lincoln, also the Conservative European Parliamentary Candidate for Staffordshire West and Congleton in June 1994. He is a councillor in the London Borough of Ealing where he is just one of two Conservatives 'in' the administration as scrutiny committee vice-chair. Has also been the Conservative Group deputy leader. An Institute of Public Relations member, he has won an award for work spanning Brussels, Whitehall and Westminster on behalf of a trade association.

Browne, Jeremy

Account Director, Corporate and Public Affairs, Edelman, London

Graduate of Nottingham University and President of the Students' Union. Worked as parliamentary assistant to Alan Beith MP, and contested the Enfield Southgate constituency in the 1997 election, standing against Michael Portillo MP. Became Director of Press and Broadcasting for the Liberal Democrats, working closely with Charles Kennedy and Paddy Ashdown. Previously worked at Dewe Rogerson and joined Edelman in May 2000.

Brunson, Michael

Associate, Luther Pendragon

A 35-year career in broadcasting began with the BBC in 1964. Joined ITN in 1968, shortly after the creation of the News at Ten. In 1973, he was appointed ITN's Washington correspondent where he covered Watergate and the 1976 presidential elections. Returning to the UK in 1977, from 1980-86 he was ITN's diplomatic editor. In 1986 he became ITN's political editor reporting on every recent political event in Britain. Covered five general elections, and awarded the Royal Television Society's Judges Award for lifetime achievment in April 2000. Has served as chairman of both the Parliamentary Lobby Journalists (1994) and the Parliamentary Press Gallery (1999). During 1998 he was a member of the Government's Advisory Group on Citizenship Education, and later served on the Preparation for Adult Life Group at the Qualifications and Curriculum Authority.

Bruce, Alastair

Director, Probus Bruce Naughton Wade

Graduate of Oxford Unversity (Classics). From 1985-1987 worked in Washington DC managing trade policy issues for IBM. Became responsible for public affairs strategy for IBM UK. Set up Bruce Naughton Wade in 1991. Serves on the Cultural Affairs Committee of the English-Speaking Union and on the Board of Trustees of the National Botanic Garden of Wales, and is Chairman of the Barnes Music Society.

Bruce, Ian

Chairman, Ian Bruce Associates Ltd

Educated at Bradford University and Mid Essex Technical College. Worked for Pye, Sainsburys, Philips, Sinclair and Edward Scientific Instruments. Started his own recruitment and management consultancy company now known as Ian Bruce Associates. Member of Parliament for South Dorset from 1987 until 2001 following a Labour gain of just 0.2%. Previously fought Burnley in 1983 and for a European Parliamentary seat for West Yorkshire in 1984. Member of Information Select Committee; President of Conservative Technology Forum; Vice Chairman of Conservative Education and Employment Back Bench Committee. Renumerated Parliamentary Adviser to Trevor Gilbert & Associates and Communications Managment Association. Chairman and Director EURIM Ltd (unpaid).

Bruce, Stuart

Chief PR Guru, Networx

Worked for the Labour Party where he was responsible for developing a regional corporate relations strategy. UK Head of Public Relations and Public Affairs Grant Thornton before setting up Networx in 1998. A Leeds City Councillor.

Burrell, Michael

Vice Chairman, Grayling Group

Graduate of St Peter's College, Oxford. Began career as a journalist and was for 10 years lobby correspondent for the Westminster Press Newspaper Group. Founded Westminster Strategy in 1986 and has held various senior positions within European Strategy and the Grayling Group. Served as Chairman of the APPC from June 1999 and reappointed in 2001 for a third and final year. Westminster Strategy represent one of the largest members of the APPC.

Butler, Alan

Director, BKSH UK

Graduate of Trinity College, Dublin (Intellectual Property Law), Cambridge and the EIU in Florence. Intern at DG 1V of the European Commission specialising in the competition aspects of information, communication and multi-media sectors. Began his career in public affairs as an adviser to Southern Electric International on the acquisition of SWEB, the first foreign takeover of a privatised UK utility. Joined GJW in 1995 and became Senior Account Executive, eventually going on to lead the City & Finance division before joining APCO UK as a Director. Upon joining APCO, performed a number of senior management functions as well as leading the Financial Services, Privatisations and TMT practices.

Butler, Arthur

Board Member, CSM Parliamentary and European Consultants Ltd

Former political correspondent of the *Daily Express* and *Daily Sketch*. Managing Director of Partnerplan Public Affairs before joining John Addey Associates. Became Joint Managing Director (with Evie Soames) of Charles Barker Watney and Powell. Secretary to the Parliamentary and Scientific Community until 1995. Joint Managing Editor of Science in Parliament until 1998. Founding Secretary of the All Party Motor Industry Group 1978-90 and the Parliamentary Information Technology Committee. Liveryman of the Worshipful Company of Tobacco and Pipe Makers and a Freeman of the City of London.

Butler, Chris

Founding Director, Butler Kelly

Chris Butler was a market research consultant before joining the Conservative Research Department 1977-1980. Worked in the Political Office at No. 10 Downing Street 1980-83, then as Special Adviser to the Secretary of State for Wales 1983-85, and Special Adviser to the Minister for the Arts and Libraries 1986-87. Market research consultant 1985-86 and Conservative MP for Warrington 1987-92 and Secretary to the Backbench Trade and Industry Committee.

Butterwick, Keith

Associate Director, PPS Group

Former Labour Councillor in Calderdale, and founder of Finance North and Northern Business & Finance magazines. Joined PPS in June 2000.

Byfield, Stephen

Managing Director, PPS Group

After working for a Labour MP and Democrat Congressman in America, he began work in public affairs. In the late 1980s he was a Director of Profile Political Communications which he left in 1990 to set up PPS with Charles St George. Took over as Group Managing Director in 2001.

Byrne, Cathy

Associate Director, Corporate and Public Affairs, Edelman, London

Graduate of Edinburgh University (Politics), and the London School of Public Relations (diploma in Public Relations). During the 1997 General Election, assisted in the re-election campaigns of the Rt. Hon. Chris Smith and Barbara Roche MP. Has been employed as a researcher for the Rt. Hon. David Blunkett MP, Secretary of State for Education and Employment, and Mrs. Barbara Roche MP, now Minister of State, Home Office. Worked for Wesminster Strategy before joining Edelman almost five years ago.

Byrne, Colin

Joint CEO, Weber Shandwick UK

Student newspaper editor and campaign officer of the National Union of Students. Former Labour Party Press Officer under Neil Kinnock. Formerly head of Shandwick's European Public Affairs practice.

Cantley, Heather

European Account Director, Central Lobby Consultants

Worked at Central Lobby Consultants since 1991. Prior to this, she worked at the European Commission and a Brussels based European Affairs Consultancy. Fluent in French, German and Dutch.

Cartwright, Rod

Director, GCI Political Counsel; Board Director, GCI London

Graduate of the University of Newcastle Upon Tyne (Modern Languages and International Political Economy). Worked as an Account Executive at PS Communications in Edinburgh and as a consultant in the Transport and Construction Unit of GJW Government Relations. Events Anchor for Tony Blair and John Prescott's on-the-road teams at the Labour Party's Millbank HQ during the 1997 General Election. In 1997, joined Politics International as Head of Transport, later becoming Head of Financial Services and Business Development Director. Left to start up GCI's public affairs arm in 1999.

Challoner, Alex

Corporate, Environment & Transport - Public Affairs Division, Golin/Harris Ludgate

Graduate of Southampton University (Law). Post graduate degree in journalism. Former National Secretary of the Tory Reform Group, Cabinet Broadcast Officer at the Conservative Central Office for the 1997 Gerneral Election and past Branch Chairman of the Putney Conservative Association. Since 1994 he was a senior consultant at lobby shop, GPC, and joined Golin/Harris Ludgate in 1998.

Ohambre, Will

Client Director, Stormont Strategy

Parlimentary assistant to three backbench MPs and was a member of the British Gas Parliamentary Affairs team during the passage of the Gas Act 1995 In 1996, appointed Assistant Director to the Future of Europe Trust (FET), based in the House of Commons where he was directly answerable to a cross-party group of MPs. Parliamentary Advisor to the Fire and Safety Development Group before spending two years with CSM Parliamentary Consultants. Joined Stormont Strategy in April 2000.

Child, Susan

Senior Policy Consultant, August. One Public Affairs

Graduate of Royal Holloway College (History). Worked in Parliament for the Social Democratic Party from 1987-92 running their Whips Office in the House of Commons and providing research for the Social Democrat Peers. Took up a position in the Research Unit of IGA in 1992, before leaving to co-found AS Biss, a specialist public affairs consultancy in 1996, where her clients included ASDA, Kingfisher and Cadbury Schweppes. She is the author of the *Politico's Guide to Parliament*.

Clarke, Nigel

Managing Director, Weber Shandwick | GJW

Research Assistant to Tom King MP 1981-82 and a researcher for the Special Programmes Unit of the CBI. Head of the Home Affairs Section and then the Political Section of the Conservative Research Department before joining GJW. Finance Director at GJW/BSMG with extensive experience in Central and Eastern Europe. Took over as Managing Director of the newly merged Weber Shandwick | GJW at the end of 2001.

Clement-Jones, Tim (Lord)

Chairman, DLA Upstream

Graduate of Trinity College, Cambridge. Former Group Company Secretary and Legal Adviser to Kingfisher plc and played a key role in its Sunday Trading Campaign. Awarded the CBE in 1988. Founding partner of Independent Corporate Mentoring, ICM, the legal management consultancy. From its inception until its sale to Lopex plc in April 1999, he was a director of Political Context. Elevated to the Lords in 1998. Chairman of Environmental Context, the environmental strategy and communications consultancy, and also a Liberal Democrat working peer and a former Chariman of the Liberal Party. Co-founding Partner of Independent Corporate Mentoring. Has been Chairman of the Association of Liberal Lawyers and was Director of the Lib-Dem Euro Campaign 1992-94.

Cockburn, Charles

Principal, Portcullis Research

Previously lecturer in government and politics in Canada and the UK. Founding Editor, *Financial Regulation Review* (subsequently bought out by the Financial Times). Worked for two UK government relations consultancies including Charles Miller's Public Policy Unit as Senior Consultant and Head of Reserch. Founded Portcullis Research in 1989. Member of the Institute of Directors.

Commons, John

Consultant, Political Intelligence

Elected to Manchester City Council in 1985. Has been a political consultant to the Association of Liberal Democrat Councillors and a parliamentary agent for five years to the Rt. Hon. Alan Beith MP. Deputy leader of the Official Opposition (Liberal Democrats) and spokesperson on Arts and Leisure, Licensing and Catering Management. Also deputy chair of the Local Government Association (LGA) Leisure and Tourism Committee and vice-chair of the LGA Policy Focus Group on Sport. Regular guest lecturer at Manchester Metropolitan University and worked as a project officer for the Liberal Democrats and Westminster Foundation for Democracy in Bosnia Herzeovina where he was stationed in Sarajevo.

Convery, Jane

Assistant Director, Saltire Public Affairs

Formerly a lecturer for four years at the University of Edinburgh, specialising in constitutional and human rights law. Author of 'The Governance of Scotland - A Saltire Guide'.

Coote, Anna

Deputy Director, Institute for Public Policy Research; Advisory Board member Probus BNW

Formerly a Senior Lecturer in Media and Communications at Goldsmith's College, London University. Deputy Editor of the *New Statesman*, in 1993 appointed Paul Hamlyn Fellow at IPPR.

Courage, Marcus

Weber Shandwick | GJW

Manages Weber Shandwick's International Government Relations programme and is Head of International

Government Affairs of Weber Shandwick's Africa practice. Sits on the Conservative Foreign and Commonwealth Council and is a member of the Royal Institute for International Affairs.

Craig, Kevin

UK Account Director, DLA Upstream

Former Research Assistant to Rt Hon John Denham MP. Between 1996 and 1999 he was an Account Director with the Rowland Company. He holds a senior elected position in London local Government.

Craven, Michael

Partner, Lexington Communications

Worked for John Prescott for most of the 1980s. Managing Director of Market Access until March 1997. Advised the then Deputy Prime Minister, John Prescott, on the transport White Paper in 1998. Former Managing Director of GPC, co-formed Lexington Communications in 1998 with Ian Kennedy. Helped to run Peter Mandelson's abortive campaign to join Labour's NEC in 1997.

Crawford, Stuart

Director of Political and Corporate Affairs, The Communication Group Scotland

Background in the Armed Forces, as author of the Army in Scotland's corporate communications strategy. Candidate in the Scottish Parliamentary Elections in 1999 and was a Prospective Parliamentary Candidate in the UK 2001 Election.

Crine, Simon

Director, APCO UK

Formerly General Secretary of the Fabian Society for six years building close contacts with senior members of the Labour Party. Mirrored New Labour's modernisation within the Fabians. Then moved to being senior consultant at Opinion Leader Research. Is now APCO's senior adviser on Government and Labour Party affairs.

Cunningham, Amanda

Director, Politics International

Joined Politics International in 1994, following a career in publishing and joined the Board in 2000.

Dardis, Eoin

Public Affairs Manager, The Waterfont Partnership

Joined as a graduate trainee in 1997, having gained a degree in Politics and International Relations.

Davies, Michael

Financial Services - Public Affairs Division, Golin/Harris Ludgate

Graduate of Buckingham University (Economics). Joined the consultancy as a graduate trainee in 1993. Focussed on financial services issues.

De Bony, Elizabeth

Director, BKSH Europe

Former journalist for Busines Europe and International Data Group News Service, publishers of *Computer World*, *Le Monde Informatique* and 200 other technology focused publications around the world.

DeLuca, Nicholas

Managing Director, APCO UK

Graduate of Rutgers University, Postgraduate research on the UK lobbying industry at Oxford University. Worked with Senator Edward Kennedy in the United States Senate, before moving to the UK as an advisor to Harry Greenway MP. Worked in the consultancy industry for 10 years, with particular experties in aviation, entertainment and leisure sectors. Founding Director of APCO UK.

Derrane, Mary

Senior Counsellor, Chelgate

Joined Chelgate in 1999 after 15 years at Pfizer Limited, where she was responsible for media relations and was editior of the company's in-house magazine. Has also been a Labour member of Thanet District Council for the past eight years, where she is the Cabinet member responsible for housing. Previously she has chaired its Economic Development & Regeneration Committee. Works in Chelgate's Local Government Unit.

Dixon, Maria

Consultant, Commonwealth Consultants Bureau

Managing Director of ISM Shipping Solutions. Advises CCB on maritime strategies, ports privitisation, brokerage, pollution response and other maritime issues. Liased with a number of government agencies. Formerly Head of Shipping at the Panamanian Consulate. Member of the Steering Committee at the IMIF London, the Indian Maritime Association (UK), and a UK Board Member of the Women's International Shipping and Trading Association.

Dobrin, Josie

Senior Consultant, Lexington Communications

Joined Lexington Communications at the end of 2000 from Luther Pendragon.

Docherty, Stephen

Associate Director, Edelman

Graduate of the University of Surrey (Drama and English Literature). Spent four years as Parliamentary Assistant and press officer to Janet Anderson MP. He also managed Janet Anderson's campaign during the 1997 General Election. Joined Weber Shandwick where he acted as media relations advisor to the Corporation of London and the Crown Estate. Has acted as PR advisor to, and spokesperson for, the Bar Council for England and Wales. Left Weber Shandwick to spearhead Edelman's new Legal and Litigation division.

Donoghue, Helen

Managing Director, Central Lobby Consultants

Graduate of London University. Joined the Bank of England management scheme. Subsequently became researcher in the House of Commons. In 1981, ran the press office of a major charity. Founded Central Lobby Consultants in 1984.

Duncan, Peter

Partner, Quadrant

Worked for a number of years as principal press officer in Whitehall. Responsible for setting up the Welsh Development Agency's press and public relations unit.

Dunlop, Andrew

Managing Director, Politics International

Started his career in international banking before joining the Conservative Research Department first as an adviser on Trade and Industry matters, and then as Head of its Political Section. Went on to become Special Adviser to the Secretary of State for Defence and adviser to the Prime Minister as a member of the Downing Street Policy Unit. Has served as a Director of the APPC.

Eastoe, Susan

Chief Operating Officer, Westminster Strategy

Formerly secretary to the All-Party Disablement Group. Member of the Government Affairs panel of the Public Relations Consultants Association, a member of the Commonwealth Society and the Institute of Directors. Formerly Chief Executive of Profile Communications.

Eisenhammer, John

Founder, Quiller Consultants

Completed a doctorate in French politics at Oxford University in 1983 after taking a First in Politics, Philosophy and Economics at Christ Church. Began career as a journalist with *Business* magazine, and then a current affairs commentator at the BBC World Service. A founder member of the *Independent*, his last position was that of Financial Editor, reporting and commenting on all aspects of the City. Spent five years for The Independent in Germany, from 1989 to 1994, first in Bonn as general correspondent, then in Frankfurt, where he concentrated on European business. In his first year he won the foreign correspondents' award for his coverage of German unification. Became The Independent's European Affairs Editor and then diplomatic correspondent. Before founding Quiller Consultants, John worked as a Senior Consultant at one of the UK's leading communications groups.

Elsen, Richard

Executive Director & Chief Political Counsel, Cicero Consulting

Began PR experience handling media relations for the West Coast main line of British Rail. Became the UK's Labour Party press officer for the West Midlands in 1993, before becoming a senior press officer for Labour's London and South East region. Joined Labour's 'Key Seats Unit' in 1996 and became Deputy Head of the

'Rebuttal & Attack' media team before and during the 1997 General Election. Became Deputy Managing Director of public affairs for Ludgate Communications in 1997 and left in 2000 to co-found Cicero Consulting.

Evans, Ceri

Managing Director - Public Affairs, Golin/Harris Ludgate

Creative Director at Channel Four, then worked for BBC News and Current Affairs, before becoming Chief of Staff and Campaign Director for Steve Norris in his London Mayoral Campaign. Recently has worked for William Hague, specialising in media briefing, message development, research and polling.

Fane-Saunders, Terence

Chairman and Chief Executive, Chelgate

Graduate of Cambridge (Law and English). Spent several years as Managing Director of Hill and Knowlton Asia Limited, during which time he also opened the first foreign public relations business in the People's Republic of China. Served on the worldwide board of Hill and Knowlton Inc, at the time the world's largest public relations company, managing 22 Hill and Knowlton offices in Asia, Latin America, Canada, Australia and New Zealand. Moved to become Chairmand and Chief Executive of Burson-Marsteller, one of the three largest public relations firms in the UK. In 1988, he founded Chelgate.

Findlay, Martin

Non-Executive Director, Whitbread; Advisory Board member, Probus BNW

Also trustee of the Baring Foundation and Chairman of the London Education Business Partnership. Has been a Non-Executive Director of the Boddington Group and Devenish Plc.

Finney, Nicholas, OBE

Managing Director, The Waterfront Partnership

Former Director General of the British Ports Federation, led the campaign for the abolition of the Dock Labour Scheme and for the privatisation of the Public Trust Port Authorities. Member of the UK's Competition Commission from 1993-99. Currently a member of the International Association of Maritime Economists and of the policy committee of the Institute of Transport and Logistics in the UK. He formed the Waterfront Partnership in 1993. Also founder and Managing Directory of The Waterfront Conference Company.

Fossey, Nathan

The Public Affairs Company

Formerly worked with Simon Hughes MP and with the Parliamentary Information Unit.

Fox, Dan

Senior Consultant, GPC London

Former assistant to Tony Blair and was part of the Labour Party's e-Campaigns in the 2001 Election. Worked for GPC London in 1998 before moving to GPC Brussels, and being seconded to the corporate affairs office of 3i.

Fraser, Jeremy

Associate Director, Weber Shandwick | GJW

Worked in the office of the Rt Hon Harriet Harman MP and served as her agent in 1992. Also worked with Tessa Jowell on local issues. Sat on the old Lewisham and North Southwark Health Authority as a local authority representative, becoming Vice Chair in 1990. Also became Chair of the local FHSA, standing down in 1994. Four years as Leader of the London Borough of Southwark, and as Labour Parliamentary Candidate he came close to unseating Simon Hughes in North Southwark and Bermondsey.

Gairdner, Andrew

Chairman, Connect Public Affairs

Qualified with Coopers and Lybrand in 1963 and has been self-employed since 1979. Founder director and shareholder of the public affairs company Market Access, and acted as its Group Finance Director from 1984 to 1994. Following aquisition by Omnicom, Andrew became the Group Chief Executive of Market Access International and later Chairman of the GPC Market Access Group. Moved to become Chairman of Connect Public Affairs when the company gained its independence from Omnicom. Acts as a director for a Granville Group subsidiary in the the City. Also acted as a trustee for a number of charities, notably as Treasurer of the National Asthma Campaign.

Galbraith, Jeremy

Chief Executive, BKSH Europe

Graduate of Leeds University (Law). Started career in the House of Commons working for Dr Keith Hampson MP, a senior member of the Trade and Industry Select Committee. Then joined Market Access, rising to Deputy Managing Director, and a Director of its sister company in Brussels. Moved to Burson-Marsteller in June 1995 to head their UK Public Affairs Practice. Established BKSH in Europe in July 1999. He fought for a London seat for the Conservative Party in the 1992 General Election. National Vice-Chairman, Conservative Friends of Israel, 1990 to date.

Gammell, Elizabeth

Business Development Director, Campaign Information

Also acts as senior consulting adviser to a number of LOBBYcontact clients. Board member of Campaign Information.

Gansler, John

Director of European Affairs, The Waterfront Partnership

Spent three years in Brussels on secondment to the European Commission's Directorate-General for Transport, also serving as Secretary to the European Port Working Group. Previously Private Secretary to the junior Minister for Transport. A 25-year long career with DETR and its predecessors included responsibility for primary and secondary legislation and implementation of EU legislation. Heavily involved in the reform of pilotage carried out by the Pilotage Act 1987.

Garrett, Nicola

Account Executive and Head of Policy, Research and Information Unit, PR21

Graduate of the University of Glamorgan (Government Affairs). Worked in the political intelligence unit of Citigate Public Affairs and as political researcher for GMTV's The Sunday Programme. Previously worked for the Welsh Local Government Association's European division. Joined PR21 in 2000.

George, Malcolm

Deputy Managing Director, Connect Public Affairs

Worked in the City for eight years for a number of international banks including Deutsche Bank. Joined Beaumark in 1994, specialising in financial services issues. At the beginning of 1997 joined GPC Connect and, later that year, became a member of the management buy-out team which created Connect Public Affairs. Emphasis not only on commercial clients but assisting 'not-for-profit' client accounts.

George, Rebecca

Head of Influence Relations, August.One

Began her career at PA Consulting, then spent five years at Paragon Communications. Moved to Text 100 as an associate director before joining August.One.

Gibbons, Jo

Associate Director, Edelman

Graduate of the University of East Anglia (Economic and Social Studies) Worked in the Labour Party's media unit in the run up to the successful 1997 election, as a media manager for MSF, the union for skilled and professional people. Then worked for the Football Association where she managed the media relations for the bid to host the 2006 World Cup. Following this, joined the Cabinet Office where she acted as special adviser to senior Cabinet Minister, Margaret Jay, Leader of the House of Lords and Minister for Women. Then joined the Prime Minister's press team for the successful 2001 election campaign. Joined Edelman in August 2001

Gibson, Mike

Senior Conference Writer, The Waterfront Partnership

Formerly a Labour Councillor on the London Borough of Southwark from 1980-1998, he was also Railtrack's External Affairs Manager for five years. He joined The Waterfront Partnership in January 2000.

Gillford, Paddy (Lord)

Chairman, The Policy Partnership

Educated at Eton and Sandhurst (Coldstream Guards). Started his career with Hanson plc. Seconded to the Home Office to advise the Rt Hon Douglas Hurd CBE, the then Home Secretary. Returned to Hanson to become a manager of their public affairs unit until joining Ian Greer Associates, 1990-93. Set up the Westminster Policy Partnership in 1993, which was renamed The Policy Partnership in 1996. Elected for two consecutive four-year terms as councillor in the Royal Borough of Kensington & Chelsea (1990-98), Chairman of Traffic & Highways Committee. Founding Chairman of the Association of Professional Political Consultants. Has advised on well over 150 mergers and aquisitions in the UK and Europe where there have been major political and public interest concerns. Holds Directorship of a number of Investment Trusts. Author of the 'Handbook of World Development' (1982).

Good, Anthony

Chairman, Flagship Group

Founder of first publically quoted PR consultancy, Good Relations. Spent five years with Silver City Airways Ltd. Non-executive positions include Arcadian plc, Care First Group plc and The International Hotel Management Servcies Ltd.

Gordon, Richard

Managing Director, Stormont Strategy

Director of CBI Northern Ireland, lobbying government and politicians on behalf of local business. Became Public Affairs Director of Short Brothers plc, the largest manufacturing company in Northern Ireland for ten years. Left to set up GCC Stormont Strategy at the end of 1994. Currently Council Member of the Northern Ireland Chamber of Commerce and Industry, and until recenty was a Council Member of the Federation of Small Businesses. Presently Chairman of the Employers' Liason Committee of the RFCA.

Gorlov, Alison

Partner and Parliamentary Agent, Winckworth Sherwood

Articled Sherwood & Co; qualified 1975; partner and parliamentary agent 1978; joined Winckworth & Pemberton 1991. Member of the Law Society, the City of Westminster Law Society and the Solicitors' Benevolent Association. Specialises in constitutional law, infrastructure projects, statutory and other companies, public sector and former public sector bodies, financial institutions and local authorities.

Gover, Mark

Senior Counsellor, Chelgate

Started career as Campaigns Manager for the British Road Federation during the Newbury Bypass Controversy and is author of the BRF reports 'Roads to Ports', and 'Signing, A Case for Change'. Moved to being responsible for public relations at the Construction Industry Training Board during their quinquennial government review. Joined Chelgate from Lantra, the National Training Organisation for land-based industries, where he was the senior manager with responsibility for corporate communications and marketing. Originally a member of the Liberal Democrats Federal Executive, Chairman of the Student Liberal Democrats and Party Agent for Windsor and Maidenhead, in 1994 he joined the Labour Party. Worked in Millbank Tower in 1997, and was Secretary to the Labour Initiative in Co-operation.

Grant, Gavin

European Chairman of Public Affairs, Burson-Marsteller

Graduate of Reading University (Political Science). Elected President of the University Student's Union. Worked for the then Liberal Leader David Steel at the time of the formation of the alliance with the SDP led by Roy Jenkins and subsequently David Owen. Stood for UK Parliament in 1983 and 1987. Ran the Liberal

Democrat Leader's National Election Tour in 1992 and 1997 and was part of the Liberal Democrats European Election Strategy team in 1994. Director of Public Affairs for the Association of Unit Trusts and Investment Funds and a former Director of Campaigns for the RSPCA. Worked as Director of Public Affairs and Communications at The Body Shop. Joined Burson-Marsteller early in late 1999.

Greenwood, Berkeley

Managing Director, Advance Communications

Graduate of the University of Liverpool (Economics). Worked with the Conservative Research Department (Housing, Transport and Arts Desk Officer) until 1988. Researcher at Public Policy Consultants (1988-1991). Fought Liverpool Walton by-election for the Conservatives in 1991, and in 1992 General Election. From 1991-91, Senior Account Executive at CSM until founded Advance Communications in 1992. MD of Advance Communications (sister company of Portcullis Research) and from 1995 Director of Healthcare at Portcullis Research.

Grender, Olly

Director, APCO UK

Researcher and speechwriter for Paddy Ashdown before becoming Director of Communications for the Liberal Democrats. Moved to position as Director of Communications at Shelter, heading a 40 strong department before joining LLM Communications in 1999. Ran the company's Strategic Communications Unit before joining APCO UK as a Director. Also serves as a Director of the APPC.

Grimley, John

Senior Counsellor, Chelgate

A native Californian, trained in the legal and political structure of the European Union at Sciences Po in Paris, and as an American lawyer. Campaign experience includes work on the US presidential campaigns of George Bush in 1992 and Bob Dole in 1996, as well as the most recent California Governors' race in 1998. Served as a writer in the George Bush White House and worked in the United States Congress and the California Legislature. Worked as Campaign Director for London-based New Europe, the pro-EU anti-euro campaign chaired by David Owen. Joined Chelgate in June 2001.

Grogan, Rosemary

Deputy Chairman, APCO UK

Head of the Parliamentary Information Service at the House of Commons Library from 1979-1985 where she advised MPs on a range of matters relating to their parliamentary duties. Founding director of Westminster Strategy in 1986. Left in 1995 to co-found APCO UK. Among major achievements was heading the team which won the PR Week award for the Best Public Affairs Campaign of 1999 working with one of the UK's major trade unions.

Hagg, Ian

Associate Director, Hill and Knowlton Public and Corporate Affairs

Background working for organisations such as the National Council for Voluntary Organisations and World Vision UK. Worked with Shell, expanding their Public Affairs capabilities across their UK business areas.

Currently Chairman of Trustees for the UK NGO TRAID that raises over £2million p/a to finance development projects in the third world.

Hall, Damien

Account Director, Central Lobby Consultants
Worked at the European Commission prior to joining Central Lobby Consultants in 1998.

Hamilton, Peter

Managing Director, The Communication Group

Harman, David

Account Executive, Political Intelligence
Graduate of Leeds University (Politics and European Parliamentary Studies) and the University of Leeds School of International, Development and European Studies (MA). Assistant to Glyn Ford MEP. Back in London, worked in the social inclusion unit of the Departmen of Education and Employment and then for the Insolvency Service.

Hatcher, Mark

Head of UK Public Affairs, PricewaterhouseCoopers.
Qualified as a barrister and worked as a UK Civil Servant, joined the Strategy and Economics practice of Coopers & Lybrand. Founded the firm's public affairs consulting practice in 1993. Following the merger with Price Waterhouse in 1998, was appointed Head of UK Public Affairs of PricewaterhouseCoopers. Appointed to the firm's Global Regulatory Affairs Board in 2000, and took on a global public affairs responsibility advising on strategic communications with governments and regulators, particularly in the area of global trade policy. Member of the Advisory Board of the Centre for Corporate and Public Affairs and the Editorial Boards of the *Journal of Communication Management* and the *Journal of Public Affairs*.

Hayes, Neil

Assistant Director, GJW/BSMG
Career started as a journalist, including a period as a Parliamentary journalist with the Press Association. Entered the Government Information and Communications Service, working across several departments, including the Home Office, MAFF and the former Department of Energy, where he was Head of Information. Spent two periods of secondment to the Prime Minister's Press Office at No. 10 Downing Street, and was the Public Affairs Adviser to the first Gas Industry Regulator Sir James McKinnon. Became Head of Corporate Media Relations and then Head of International Public Affairs at British Gas, after the 1992 election. Joined GJW/BSMG in 1999.

Heald, Gordon

Managing Director, The Opinion Research Business
Former Managing Director of Social Surveys (Gallup Poll), established ORB in 1994.

Hepton, Sally

Account Manager, LLM Communications

Has worked on several Conservative election campaigns, including the London Mayoral campaign. Before joining LLM Communications, she was Marketing Executive at the *House Magazine*.

Hill, Jonathan CBE

Founder, Quiller Consultants

Graduate of Trinity College, Cambridge (Double First in History). Initial spell in Whitehall from 1986 - 89, when he worked as a Special Adviser in three Government Departments - Employment, Health and Trade and Industry. Then a four-year spell at 10 Downing Street, first in the Policy Unit (1991-92) and then as Political Secretary and Head of the Prime Minister's Political Office (1992-94). In the Policy Unit, specialised in transport, housing and inner city policy. As Political Secretary, ran the Prime Minister's campaign during the 1992 General Election. He left Downing Street in December 1994 to join Lowe Bell Consultants. Founder of Quiller Consultants in 1998. Written, with Baroness Hogg, an account of life at 10 Downing Street entitled 'Too Close To Call'. On the Boards of the National Literacy Trust and Crime Concern, a member of the Steering Group of the Museum of British History, and is a Governor of Highgate School.

Hopkins, Jonathan

Director of Public Affairs, PR21

Undertook research and policy work for the Labour Party Front Bench teams on environmental and transport issues following the 1987 General Election. Political Adviser to Doug McAvoy, General Secretary of the National Union of Teachers, responsible for campaigns development from 1991-95. Director of IGA from 1995-96 and joined the Board of PR21 in 1996 to head up public affairs. Received the Institute of Public Relations Sword of Excellence Award for not-for-profit organisations in 1999.

Hughes, Bernard

Director of Public Affairs, Edelman, London

Started his career with the British Retail Consortium. Joined Edelman from Tesco Plc where he created a Government and Public Policy Unit before becoming the European Public Affairs Manager. Represented Tesco on the multinational European Retail Round Table. Also worked for the European Commission, developing ideas to promote European business competitiveness, and played a prominent role in defending supermarkets in the recent Competition Commission enquiry.

Hutchinson, George

Associate Director, Weber Shandwick | GJW

Graduate of Manchester University (Economics and Politics). Advised McDonald's Restaurants while they were involved in the BSE crisis and the longest running court case in UK legal history.

Hutt, Tony

Associate Director, Weber Shandwick | GJW

Worked at the Conservative Research Department from 1971 to 1984 for much of the time as Desk Officer responsible for local government. Responsible for Housing, Education, Environment, Arts and Sports desks before becoming Head of the Home Affairs section. Served as member of Luton Borough Council from 1973 to 1976 where he was opposition spokesman on planning. Joined GJW/BSMG in 1984.

Irving, Paul

Partner and Parliamentary Agent, Winckworth Sherwood

Graduate of Trinity College, Oxford (1979 BA Classics; 1984 MA; 1987 DPhil). Called to the Bar, Middle Temple (1986), pupillage in Chancery Chambers. Articled Sherwood & Co, qualified 1991; partner Winckworth Sherwood since 1992. Specialises in drafting, promoting and advising on legislation with particular emphasis on transport, ports, utilities, compulsory purchase and planning.

Jacobs, Ilan

Account Director, Consolidated Communications

Former researcher to Peter Mandelson, working on Mandelson's definitive book on New Labour, 'The Blair Revolution'. Ilan also assisted Philip Gould, Labour's senior campaign strategist during the 1997 campaign, before joining the public affairs consultancy Lawson Lucas Mendelsohn. Joined Consolidated Communications as Account Manager in April 1999.

James, Mari

Director, Weber Shandwick | GJW

Leading member of the National Assembly Advisory Group and the Assembly Preparations Group, whose recommendations became the blueprint for the structures and procedures of the Assembly. Also Vice-Chair of the Yes for Wales referendum in 1997.

Jarman, Richard,

Account Director, Consolidated Communications

Graduate of Oxford University (History). Practised as a solicitor before working as a House of Commons researcher to Labour MPs Margaret Hodge and Stephen Twigg, and as parliamentary officer for a national disability organisation. Also formerly Head of Public Affairs at the Commission for Racial Equality where he played a key role in the lobbying activity surrounding the Race Relations (Amendment) Act 2000. Labour councillor in the London Borough of Lambeth with special responsibility for schools and equal opportunities. Works in a voluntary capacity for Baroness Howells of St. David's on behalf of the Stephen Lawrence Charitable Trust.

John, Steve, Dr

Head of Policy, PPS Public Affairs

Ph.D. from the LSE on 'The Effectiveness of Professional Lobbying'. Worked as Politics and Finance Producer for ITN, and Political Analyst on the Channel Tunnel Rail Link, involved in all aspects of the legislative programme. Consultancy experience includes work at the Public Policy Unit and GJW Government Relations.

Johnson, Graham

Director, Flagship Group

Graduate of Cambridge University (Political Philosophy and Social Psychology). Worked at the Ministry of

Defence, Department of Education and the Cabinet Office before working as a consultant by Coopers & Lybrand. Before joining Rosehaugh plc. where Dick Newby, another Director of the Flagship Group was working.

Jones, Bill

Associate Director, Weber Shandwick | GJW

Graduate of the University of York (History and Politics). Joined the Civil Service in 1988, working in several departments before a five year Foreign Office posting to the UK Permanent Representation to the European Union in Brussels. Responsible for negotiating telecoms, intellectual property and research property, working with many senior policy officials and special advisers.

Jones, Cameron

Associate Director, Weber Shandwick | GJW

Worked for the Department of the Environment, Transport and the Regions prior to joining GJW/BSMG.

Jones, Rhion

Chairman, Campaign Information

Ex-Parliamentary Candidate. 20 years experience in the IT industry. Built up the LOBBYcontact business. Acknowledged expert in Customer Relationship Management.

Kaye, Beverly

Chief Executive, PR21

Keable, Nick

Managing Director, PPS (Local & Regional)

After eight years commissioned service in the Grenadier Guards, he worked in Brussels for two conservative Members of the European Parliament, one of whom is now Leader of the British Conservative Group. He left to work for a political consultancy in Brussels and after two years returned to the UK to set up a London office before joining PPS in 1996. Elected councillor in an outer London borough in 1998.

Kelly, Phil

Director, Butler Kelly

Freelance journalist and PR consultant 1970-87. Co-founded Leveller, 1976; State Research, 1977 and edited *Tribune*, 1987-1991. He was adviser and press officer to Michael Meacher MP, then Shadow Secretary of State, Social Security and is a former Deputy Leader of Islington Borough Council. He was a Labour candidate in 1992.

Kennedy, Ian

Partner, Lexinton Communications

Former Director of GPC, co-formed Lexington Communications with Mike Craven, then the Managing Director of GPC.

Kennedy, Nigel

CEO, Grayling Group

Knowles, Robert

Consultant, Commonwealth Consultants Bureau

Graduate of St Edmund Hall, Oxford University; Institute of Education, University of London. Formerly a principal lecuturer, vocational teacher training, Garnett College and a guest lecturer, Univerisity of Technology, Sydney. Former Editor of Science and Engineering in the UK and Europe, McGraw Hill. Acts as Government/Civil Service Consultant, Education/Training including doctors, paramedics and the uniformed services.

Know, Frances

Director, Keene Public Affairs

Graduate of Warwick University (History and Politics), Post-Graduate in International Public Relations. Worked for a corporate and consumer PR company before joining Keene in 1997.

Koops, Eric

Board Member, CSM Parliamentary and European Consultants Ltd

Director of nine UK companies. Chairman of the Duke of Edinburgh's Award World Fellowships until 1998. Founding Trustee and Chairman of The Friends of Africa Foundation. Former Bow Group treasurer and Tory Party Candidate in Wakefield. Served in Margaret Thatcher's Private Office during the 1979, 1983 and 1987 election campaigns. Trustee of the Institute for Policy Research. Publications include 'Money for our Masters' (1970) and 'Airports for the Eighties' (1980).

Landa, Clive

Advisory Board Member, Probus BNW

Non-executive director of the Waltham Forest Housing Action Trust and a former Chairman of the Trustees of the Shelter Housing Action Centre. Long-standing involvement in the Conservative Party. Broad background in broadcast media and independent consultant in strategic conmmunications techniques.

Lansman, Nicholas

Managing Director, Political Intelligence

Graduate of Manchester University (Economics and Politics). Elected to represent the University at the National Union of Students' conference in 1988. Worked for the press office of the European Commission in London and then as part of a consultancy team for France Telecom and Telecom Eireann. Worked in Public Relations for the European Community in Seville at the Universal Exposition (1991-92). Co-launched Political Intelligence Ltd in 1994. Commentator on BBC Radio Berkshire and appointed Rapporteur by the European Commission's UK Representation. Chief Executive of EuroColumn, a news agency providing copy to a wide range of newspapers and journals covering European Union affairs. Fluent in English, French and Spanish.

Lawler, Geoffrey

The Public Affairs Company

Former Conservative Member of Parliament for Bradford North (1983-87), having also worked for Conservative Central Office and in a PR Consultancy. Currently also a Director of Democracy International Ltd. Vice President, International Access Inc. FCO Observer for the Russian Elections in 1993, 1995 and 1996; UN Observer for the South African Elections 1994; EU Observer in Liberia 1997. Freeman of the City of London.

Lawson, Neal

Director, LLM Communications

Former adviser to Gordon Brown MP and senior researcher at the TGWU. Ran the campaign to stop privatisation of the Post Office (winning the PR Week Campaign of the Year). Co-founded LLM in 1997.

Le Jeune, Martin

Director, Fishburn Hedges

Graduate of University College, London. Worked in marketing before joining the civil service (Cabinet Office) in 1986. Became private secretary to successive Ministers for Arts and Civil Service between 1989 and 1992. From 1992-93, head of conduct and discipline branch in the Cabinet Office, with responsibility for central rules on conduct. Seconded to National Westminster Bank for two years as head of public policy. On returning to the civil services, became the assistant secretary of the Committee on Standards in Public Life, drafting considerable sections of the first three 'Nolan Committee' reports. Joined Fishburn Hedges in 1998, working in public affairs and corporate reputation management. Became a Director in October 2000. Chair of the standards committee at the London Borough of Lambeth and a Director of the APPC.

Leathley, Arthur

Head of Communications, The Waterfront Partnership

From 1992-97, he was Political Correspondent at *The Times*, and between 1997 and 2000, he was their Transport/Aviation Correspondent. Moved to becoming their City Correspondent, before joining The Waterfront Partnership in 2001.

Lebeaux, Thierry

Citigate

Spent seven years as an economist in DGs III and XV, handling work on competition, media policy and the internal market in services and legislative drafting. Now heads Citigate's Brussels office.

Leviton, Craig

Director, LLM Communications

Formerly a Director of a number of All-Party Parliamentary Groups before becoming an Account Director with Shandwick Public Affairs. In July 1996, he provided advice to the South African High Commission on the state visit of President Mandela to the UK.

Linton, Peter

Chairman, BKSH Europe

Based in Brussels since 1972, specialising in European integration.

Lintott, Robert

Board Member, CSM Parliamentary and European Consultants Ltd

Former Managing Director of Esso Petroleum, and former Chief Executive of the Coverdale Organisation 1987-91. Executive Chairman of the Foundation for Management and Educators, and Chairman of the Governors, Queen's College, Taunton.

Lock, Stephen

Chief Executive, Cicero Consulting

Graduate of Sidney Sussex College, Cambridge (Law then Art History). Bond trading desk with Lazard Brothers & Co. Ltd. until joining Ludgate Communications in 1994. Became Managing Director of Public Affairs and in 1996, an Executive Director. Resigned from Ludgate with other Cicero founders in 2000 in order to form Cicero Consulting. Stephen Lock is a Member of the Council of Britain in Europe, the Labour Party and the Institute of Public Relations (UK).

Lowry, Roger

Manager, BKSH

Graduate of Guildhall University, London (Politics and Government), Masters Degree in Politics. From 1992-96, assistant to the current Social Security Select Committee Chairman, Archy Kirkwood MP, Liberal Democrat Welfare spokesman and Chief Whip. 1996-98, Secretary to the Parliamentary Party for the Liberal Democrats, managing their Whip's Office. Appointed by the Rt. Hon. Paddy Ashdown MP to develop and promote the Liberal Democrat's strategy on the Joint Cabinet Committee on Constitutional Reform, chaired by Rt. Hon. Tony Blair. Joined Burson-Marsteller in February 1999.

Lucas, Ben

Managing Director, LLM Communications

Head of Research and Communications at the construction trade union UCATT, before moving to become adviser to Jack Straw. Then became a senior consultant at Lowe Bell Political where he advised the financial industry. Advised Tony Blair before the 1997 election. Co-founded LLM in 1997.

Luff, Frances

Manager Head, BKSH London

Graduate of Bristol University (Russian and French). Joined the Foreign and Commonwealth Office. Following postings in Egypt and Bahrain, spent three and half years in Toronto working closely with the Department of Trade and Industry to help British exporters to Canada as Vice-Consul at the British Consulate-General. Finally worked as Private Secretary to the Minister of State at the Foreign Office before joining BKSH.

Luff, Peter

Former researcher to Peter Walker MP and then Head of Edward Heath's Private Office 1980-82. Managing Director at Good Relations 1980-87. Became a senior consultant with Lowe Bell Communications when they took over Good Relations and also acting as special adviser to the Secretary of State for Trade and Industry. Returned to Good Relations as Assisting Managing Director again until 1992. Became Conservative MP for Mid Worcester in 1992 where he has remained to date.

MacFadyen, Ian

Consultant, Commonwealth Consultants Bureau

Former civil servant, worked with Ministers in the Cabinet Office to produce Better Quality Services, the Government's former policy and guidance on reviewing and outsourcing government services. As a Health Authority Director in County Durham, engineered a purchasing consortium of local GPs and the health authority. Now a consultant in Public Service Transformation.

MacIntosh, Fiona

Associate Director, PPS Group

Graduate of Leeds University (Politics). Worked for Labour and Conservative MPs in Westminster and constituency offices. Member of the Management Committee of the Labour Planning and Environment Group. Having joined in 1994, now runs PPS Bristol.

Mack, Penny

Senior Consellor, Chelgate

Worked as a House of Commons researcher for Simon Burns MP, then Shadow Minister for Environment, Planning and Construction. Worked as a public relations and public affiars consultant to the property industry. Joined Chelgate in March 2001.

Mack, Robert

Director, BKSH Europe

Heads BKSH's team in Brussels, specialising in European Union policy and regulation.

MacLennan, Peter

Stratagem

Graduate of the University of Dundee, (MA Hons Geography and European Studies). Project Support Consultanat for the Northern Ireland Health and Social Services. Research Assistant to the Northern Ireland Labour Party during multi-party talks at Stormont.

Maggiore, Matteo

Head of European Policy, BBC

Formerly Director of Media, Telecommunications and Technology with Grayling Political Strategy. Also Deputy Director of the Television Department of the European Broadcasting Union.

Mason, Mike

Director, Connect Public Affairs

Worked for three years as a Labour Party campaign organiser. In 1993, became a policy research officer for the Labour Party's front-bench employment team in Parliament before moving to the health portfolio. Joined Market Access in August 1997, and moved to Connect Public Affairs as an Associate Director before being promoted to Director in 2000.

Massingham, David

Director, Politics International

Started his career with a campaigning environmental organisation before working as a policy adviser in local government. Later became a senior civil servant in the Departments of the Environment and Transport and the Cabinet Office. Joined Politics International as a consultant in 1995 and was appointed to the Board in 1999.

McCulloch, Ian

Senior Partner, Bircham Dyson Bell

Graduate of the University of Dundee (LLB Hons Jurisprudence and Philosophy). Admitted as a solicitor in 1976, a partner at Bircham Dyson Bell since 1977 and enrolled as a Roll 'A' Parliamentary Agent in 1979. President of the Law Society of Parliamentary Agents 1995-98. President of the City of Westminster Law Society 1994-95. Extensive experience with a wide range of public authorities and corporate and trade association clients on Parliamentary, planning and other legislative projects.

McCutcheon, Muriel

Cherton

Left a career in the Northern Ireland Civil Service to co-found Cherton, a public affairs company based in Norther Ireland, with Billy Pinkerton.

McDonald, Katherine

Stratagem

Graduate of St. John's College Oxford. Research and Press assistant to Mo Mowlam MP, the then Shadow Secretary of State for Northern Ireland. Press and Public Relations Officer for The Northern Ireland Association for the Care and Resettlement of Offenders. Joined Stratagem in 1999. Board member of the Ulster People's College. Completed the Belfast Common Purpose Programme.

McErlane, Terence

Strategem

Graduate of the University of Limerick (MA European Integration); University College Dublin (Postgraduate diploma in Business and Information Technology). Worked at the Institute for European Affairs where he was awarded a contract to vet European Legislation for the Oireachtas (The Irish Parliament). Joined Stratagem in 2000.

McIntyre, Malcolm

CMA Group

McLaren, Mark

Account Director, Central Lobby Consultants

Age Concern's government and parliamentary affairs officer prior to joining Central Lobby Consultants in 2001.

McLean, Sandy

Director, GPC London

Eleven years with Fleishman-Hillard in the USA and Europe, before joining GPC Brussels in 1999. Moved to GPC London as Director in 2001.

McLeod, Jonathan

Senior Director, Weber Shandwick | GJW

Six years in journalism before moving into public affairs in 1994.

McNicol, Shelly

Director, Morgan Allen Moore

For two years she was National Treasurer of NUS, and was Chair of the Board of NUS Services Ltd, overseeing a staff of 22 with an annual turnover of £82m. Served as director of Endsleigh Insurance. Joined Morgan Allen Moore after working in brand management with Procter & Gamble.

McRobert, Rosemary

Board Member, CSM Parliamentary and European Consultants Ltd

Former Deputy Director of the Consumers' Association. A Director of the Investors Compensation Scheme until 1996, and a member of the British Hallmarking Council until 1997.

Mendelsohn, Jon

Director, LLM Communications

Formerly an adviser to Tony Blair on business relations and campaign strategy. Also the former Secretary of the All Party Parliamentary War Crimes Group which secured the passage of the 1991 Act. Co-founded LLM in 1997.

Meyer, Lutz

CEO, Weber Shandwick Worldwide, Europe

Miller, Charles

Founded the Public Policy Unit, which became one of the most respected consultancies in the field, before merging it with Citigate Westminster to form one of Europe's largest lobbying firms, Citigate Public Affairs. Author of *Politico's Guide to Political Lobbying*.

Miller, Simon

Board Director, Hill and Knowlton Public and Corpoarate Affairs

Graduate of the University of Keele. National Youth Officer at the English Speaking Union. Rejoined Hill and Knowlton after four years as Head of Public Affairs at Railtrack, where he was responsible for the company's political communications with national and local government through privatisation, its regulatory review and for crisis communications following the Ladbroke Grove rail disaster. Fellow of the Industry and Parliament Trust.

Milton, Simon

Chairman, APCO UK

Helped launch APCO UK as Managing Director in 1995. Stood as Conservative candidate in Leicester East in the 1997 Gerneral Election and is Chariman of a Local Education Authority in London.

Moffat, Hazel

Assistant Director, Saltire Public Affairs

Qualified solicitor with experience in corporate and commercial law and government policy work, having worked on a company law reform project with the Law Commissions and the Department of Trade and Industry.

Moir, Richard

Proprietor, Commonwealth Consultants Bureau

Ineternational relations expert, issues management, specialising in the UN, WTO, EU, Commonwealth and inter-government. Wide experience in financial services, on/offshore, particularly private banking, international insurance/reinsurance, trade, multi-media, international shipping. Founder Chairman of European Film Finance and Insurance (EFFIA). Educated: Merchiston Castle, Edinburgh; York University, Toronto; LSE; Sorbonne; Institute of Political Studies, Paris; College of Insurance (UK). Hon Treasurer, 'Friends of the Bahamas'; founder member, 'Friends of Slovenia'; British–Uzbek Society, Carribbean Expo. Elected Member of Council, London Chamber of Commerce and Industry; Chartered Insurance Institute; IPR; Foreign Press Association.

Mollett, Richard

Director, PPS Public Affairs

Former Royal Naval Officer and specialises in policy analysis on transport issues. Assisted the Managent Consultancy Association with developing an All-Party Parliamentary Group and lobbying at the World Trade Organisation. Currently working on developing a public affairs campaign for the Rugby Football Union and is consultant to Energis on the development of the new telecommunications regulator, Ofcom.

Moore, Richard

Director, Morgan Allen Moore

Formerly a financial Editor of the *Royal Gazette* newspaper in Bermuda, a BBC Radio producer in London and News Editor of the *Sunday Mirror*. Twice winner of the Mirror Group Newspaper's Hugh Cudlipp Award for Outstanding Journalism. Recognised by *PR Week* for 'Best International Campaign' and the Institute of Professional Advertisers (IPA) for 'Most Effective Advertisment'.

Moore, Theo

Senior Account Manager, August.One Public Affairs

Graduate of Cambridge University (History). Joined the Corporate and Public Affairs Group at the London office of Edelman before leaving to join August.One Public Affairs in 1999.

Morgan, Steve

Managing Director, Morgan Allen Moore

Worked and taught throught West and East Europe. During the general election campaign of 1997, responsible for arranging and co-ordinating a series of nation-wide events for a number of then Shadow Ministers.

Morris, Gill

Managing Director, Connect Public Affairs

After five years working in Parliament, co-founded the specialist housing and Parliamentary consultancy, Raynsford and Morris Limited. In 1992, set up an independent consultancy practice, but was headhunted a year later to work on Government and Parliamentary relations contracts at GCI, part of GREY. Joined Connect Public Affairs in 1994 as Joint Managing Director. When the company merged with GPC Connect, now part of Omnicom, in February 1996. He headed Connnect's management buy-out team. Also heads the company's political and public affairs conference and event management unit, Connect Conferences. Member of the Steering Group of the All-Party Parliamentary Homelessness and Housing Need Group. Also a member of the Management Committee of the APPC.

Munro, Christine Stewart

Managing Director, CSM Parliamentary and European Consultants Ltd

Former Councillor for the London Borough of Camden, and researcher to backbench MPs. Former Administrative secretary to the All Party Parliamentary Group for the Chemical Industry. Founding Executive Secretary for the Parliamentary Group for Energy Studies, and founding editor of *Energy Focus*. Founding and Administrative Secretary of the All Party Parliamentary Group for Building Societies and Financial Mutuals. First woman Companion of the Institute of Energy. Sole 1995 and 1996 judge of the Public Affairs category of the Institute of Public Relations Sword of Excellence Award. Senior Vice Chairman of the Government Affairs Group. Lecturer on Parliamentary procedure. Trustee of three charities and General Commissioner of Income Taxes. Founded CSM in 1974.

Murgatroyd, Lee

Account Director, August.One

Following six years agency experience, joined August.One in 1998.

Murphy, Jackie

Director, Flagship Group

Graduated from Exeter University. Joined Good Relations where she was a director, moved to become a director of The Communication Group, and then joined Royle Communications, which subsequently became Millbank PR.

Murtagh, Pat

Political Affairs Manager, Perchards

Worked in the Press and Communications Department of one of the main political groups in the European Parliament. Joined Perchards in 1988.

Nash, David

Director, Saltire Public Affairs; Partner, Shepherd & Wedderburn

Formerly a senior government solicitor in the Scottish Office.

Simon Nayyar

Citigate Public Affairs, Executive Director

As well as being Executive Director of Citigate Public Affairs, is also a Director of Citigate Westminster Limited. Recent transactions on which he has advised have included Lloyds TSB/Scottish Widows and Whitbread/Allied Domecq/Punch Taverns. Member of the Board of the Public Relations Consultants Association (PRCA) and Chairman of its Public Affairs Committee, where he has lead the dialogue with the Wicks Committee and the Scottish Parliament.

Nicholson, David

Consultant, Butler Kelly

Former Conservative MP, served on the Commons Public Accounts and Education and Employment Select Committees; PPS to the Minister for Overseas Development; former Deputy Director-General of the British Chambers of Commerce.

Ogbogbo, Mendora

Director, Parliamentary Contacts

Graduate of Nottingham University (Politics). Worked for various media organisations before becoming a Parliamentary Researcher, then Parliamentary Officer and finally, Group Secretariat to the All Party Parliamentary Group on Ageing & Older People. Launched Paliamentary Contacts. In September 2001 Parliamentary Contacts Recruitment Agency launched its political consultancy arm during the Party political conference season, making Ms Ogbogbo the first black woman in Britain to run a Public Affairs company. Awarded European Federation of Black Women Business Owners, Young Entrepreneur Award in November 2001.

Oliver, Quintin

Managing Director, Stratagem

Graduate of St. Andrew's University and the Open University (Diploma in Management). Welfare Rights Adviser with Strathclyde Regional Council, 1980-84. Director of the Northern Ireland Council for Voluntary Action, 1985-1998. Founder and first President of the European Anti-Poverty Network, 1990-92, and Secretary, 1992-94. Appointed by President Mary Robinson to sit on the Council of State of Ireland. Board Member of Belfast-based think tank, Democratic Dialogue. Formed Stratagem, Northern Ireland's first dedicated lobbying and public affairs agency, in 1998.

Owen, Arthur

Consultant, Commonwealth Consultants Bureau

Graduate of University College, London (Physics) with a PhD in Nuclear Physics. Formerly a Director and Vice President of Booz Allen & Hamilton. Specialises in telecommunications and broadcasting, and improving critical business processes, acting as a professional adviser.

Owen, Robert

Partner and Head of Parliamentary and Public Law Department, Bircham Dyson Bell

Graduate of the University of London (BA Law and Politics). Joined Bircham Dyson Bell in 1987 and became a partner in 1991. Roll 'A' Parliamentary Agent. Experience with public works and infrastructure, particularly in the transport industry.

Page, Tony

Associate Director, Weber Shandwick | GJW

Reading Borough Councillor since 1973 and, since 1986, Chairman of Reading Transport. He is Chairman of the controlling Labour Group. From 1975-76, investigator at the newly established Commission for Local Administration. Between 1976-1980, Assistant and then Local Government Officer at Labour Party Headquarters. In 1980, Political Adviser to Gerald Kaufman, who had been appointed Shadow Environment Secretary. Transferred to the new Shadow Environment Secretary, Dr John Cunningham, in 1993.

Parr, Dawn

Account Director, Hill and Knowlton Corporate and Public Affairs

Graduate of the University of Liverpool (Ancient History, Classical Archaeology and Ancient Greek); MPhil (Marine Archaeology). Worked in the Civil Service for twelve years,, working for four Ministers under two Governments and was responsible for Competition, Consumer Affairs, Insolvency, Company Investigations, Companies House and Export Licences. Spent last five years in Civil Services as Private Secretary in the Departments of Employment and Trade & Industry.

Peel, David

Director, Weber Shandwick | GJW

Joined the senior Weber Shandwick team in early Autumn 2000 after almost 20 years as a journalist and then a civil servant in the Government Information Service. Career as a civil servant culminated in joining the press office at 10 Downing Street working with the Prime Minister and his press secretary.

Pendlington, Mark

Chief Executive, Country Landowners & Business Associates

For three years responsible for the Local Government Department at Conservative Central Office. Agent and Adviser to Lord Parkinson during his time as Party Chairman, as Trade & Industry Secretary and Energy Secretary. Worked on special projects at No. 10 Downing Street reporting to Margaret Thatcher and John Major. Moved to BAA as Group Parliamentary Affairs Manager, and in 1992 to British Gas as Director of Public Affairs. Previously worked as Director at Bell Pottinger. Joined PPS in 1999 and became Managing Director until 2001.

Pendry, Tim

Executive Chairman, Tim Pendry - Public Affairs, Public Relations, Media Relations

Senior executive in several of the largest international communications consultancies, including a major role in financial communications as lead manager for significant contested takeovers and controversies. As crisis and communications adviser, handled the Mass Privatisation Programme of the Russian Federation in 1992, the Al-Shifa bombing of 1998 and the South Iraqi Marshes Project for the AMAR International Charitable Foundation in 2001. Advised Ken Livingstone in the period during which his bid for the Mayoralty for London was being formulated, and oversaw a business communications campaign for the office of Gordon Brown in the 1992 election. Was part of the founding teams of a number of public policy think tanks in the UK, including Demos and Catalyst. Is on the Advisory Board of the Relationships Foundation and the Board of the Middle East Association.

Perchard, David

Managing Director, Perchards

Started Career with the Food Manufacturers Federation, then Cadbury Schweppes. Joined CSM Parliamentary Consultants and co-founded Perchards in 1987. From 1989-92 he was a member of the Steering Group for the Sheffield Kerbside Collection project. He was also a founder-member of the National Recycling Forum (now part of Waste Watch). Appointed Consultant to CEN, the European Committee for Standardisation in 1988. Member of several official advisory committees in the UK.

Perchard, Denise

Managing Director, Perchards

Managed a major specialised bookselling and mail order business before co-founding Perchards in 1987. Responsible for finance and administration and manages Perchards' own publications activities.

Perl, Damian

Consultant, Commonwealth Consultants Bureau

International Risk Management Consultant. Formed Global Liason Operational Backup (GLOBAL) in 1998, having worked with Defence Systems Ltd and Control Risks Group.

Pharoah, Andrew

Managing Director, Hill & Knowlton Public and Corporate Affairs division, London

Started career as an elected officer of Labour's student wing, an adviser to a local authority Labour Group and MEP, a full-time regional organiser and a national official. Moved to become Campaign Co-ordinator for the British Road Federation for three and a half years with a responsibility for national and regional campaigns, media relations and political lobbying. Joined Hill and Knowlton and was appointed to the Board of Directors in 1999. As well as being the Managing Director of their Public and Corporate Affairs division, he heads the company's cross-divisional Environment Practice. Currently serving as a Director of the APPC.

Phillips, Alison

Account Director

Initially worked as a legislative assistant in the US Congress and then worked for John Battle MP, Labour Shadow Housing Minister as research adviser and General Election campaign organiser in 1992. Moved to become Public Affairs Manager for the Design Council, and now specialises in information technology and communications industries with Hill and Knowlton.

Pinkerton, Billy

Cherton

Left a career in the Northern Ireland Civil Service to co-found Cherton, a public affairs company based in Norther Ireland, with Muriel McCutcheon.

Pitcher, George

Partner and co-founder, Luther Pendragon

Worked widely as a business and financial journalist in the national, trade and professional press, and writes a regular business column for *Marketing Week*. Formerly industrial editior of *The Observer* and in 1991 was voted National Newspaper Industrial Journalist of the Year. Co-founded Luther Pendragon in 1992 and served as the company's chief executive until the establishment of the partnership structure in 1999.

Porter, Martin, Dr

Vice-President - Consulting Services, Adamson BSMG Worldwide

Graduate of Bath University (European Studies and Modern Languages), awarded a Doctorate in 1995. He was researcher and lecturer at Bath University on the European Single Market, environmental policy and interest group representation in the EU's political process. He joined Adamson BSMG Worldwide in 1997, and is involved in establishing the Bath-Brussels society.

Prashar, Usha

Member of the Lord Chancellor's Advisory Committee on Legal Education and Conduct; Advisory Board member, Probus BNW

Director of the Runnymede Trust, 1977-84, and former Director of the National Council for Voluntary Organisations (NCVO). Non-Executive Director of Channel Four Television and of the Energy Saving Trust.

Pursey, Mark

Senior Counsellor, Chelgate

A former researcher for the Liberal Democrat Social Security Team, and handled the team's press relations during the Lone Parent Benefits debate. Moved to the Corporation of London where he was Press Spokesman for the Lord Mayor of the City of London, and co-ordinated major London events such as the Queen Mother's 100th birthday party before joining Chelgate. Has also written for the *Evening Standard*'s gossip column, 'Londoner's Diary'.

Rashbrook, Ian

Head of Parliamentary and Client Services, The Waterfront Partnership

Member of the European Parliament in the West Midlands for the Labour Party, and also worked in the Labour Party's London Regional Office during the election campaign of 1992. Worked at the Headquarters of the Associated Society of Locomotive Engineers and Fireman for seven years, before joining The Waterfront Partnership in 1999.

Relf, Aidan

Managing Director, RGMR Media and Government Relations

Started careeer as Parliamentary officer for the Association of British Insurers. Left to spend nearly ten years as a senior consultant for Burson-Marsteller and Citigate Dewe Rogerson before leaving in 1996 to set up his own consultancy. BT Cellnet and Training & Enterprise Councils' National Council followed him to RGMR. In addition to his client work, he acted as a pro bono adviser to the Maxwell Pensioners Action Group. Formerly a Parliamentary Officer for the Association of British Insurers. Member of the Institute of Public Relations.

Ricards, Sarah

Senior Associate Director, Hill and Knowlton Public and Corporate Affairs

Ten years experience working with specialist Government affairs agencies, particularly in health and social policy fields. Also worked on several high profile projects in the arts world.

Rich, Ben

Partner, Luther Pendragon

Joined Luther Pendragon in 1995, having previously been deputy director of policy with the Liberal Democrats, where he was responsible for policy development on education, constitutional and social policy, and home affairs. Also a former political researcher on Northern Ireland and author of the Liberal Democrat's 1994 European Election manifesto.

Richards, Tony

Managing Director, Keene Public Affairs

Graduate of the Universites of Sheffield (History and Politics) and Essex (American Government). Taught in the Sudan through the Voluntary Services Overseas. Four years as Director of Research for the Liberal Party before working in the House of Commons as Press and Political Secretary to the Leader. Briefly a managment consultant before being appointed as Press and Public Affairs Manager at the London Chamber of Commerce and Industry, Britain's largest Chamber of Commerce, also editing the journal *Commerce International*. Appointed Managing Director of CBA Public Affairs Ltd in 1984. Fought two General Elections at Newbury, Berkshire, in 1979 and 1983. Established Keene Public Affairs in 1986. Member of the Institute of Public Relations.

Riggins, Phil

Managing Director, SWR Europe

Received his Master's degree in political science from the American University in Washington DC in 1990, and was awarded a Presidential Management Internship in 1991. Spent five years conducting survey research for the US Information Agency across Europe and the world, including managing focus groups designed to develop a public relations campaign for the US Treasury's introduction of the new $100 bill. Joined SWR Worldwide and now runs their London office and overseas international research.

Riley, Melanie

Associate Director, Cicero Consulting

Joined corporate communications department of Nomura International plc., where she became head of Media Relations. Joined Ludgate Public Affairs in 1997 whilst concurrently working as an adviser to the Financial Services Authority on its consumer education proposals. Resigned from Ludgate in 2000 to join Cicero Consulting. Associate Member of the Institute of Public Relations and member of The IPR City and Financial Group, and was Secretary to the Committee for two years between 1994 and 1996.

Roberts, Huw

Managing Director, Strategy in Wales

Robertson, Yvonne

DLA Upstream, Scotland

Former deputy Leader of Inverclyde Council. Convenor of Corporate Business for Inverclyde Council and Labour Councillor for Bow Farm/Pennyfern ward. Headed the recent launch of DLA Upstream's move into Scotland.

Robinson, John

Vice-Chairman, BKSH

Graduate from Manchester University (French) and a Masters in Government. Founding editor of **European Report** and regularal contibutor to *The Economist, The Washington Post, Business International* and *Business Europe*. From 1981-84, served as a member of the European Commission Spokesman's Group, when he was press secretary to the Commissioner for Social Affairs, Ivor Richard. Sole editor of the master version of the Commission's book on the 1992 single market programme '1992 - The European Challenge', May 1988, and has also authored a number of other influential reports. Partner of European Research Associates for four years from 1985-89. In 1989, together with Peter Linton, he co-founded Robinson Linton Associates.

Roche, Nicholas

Consultant, Commonwealth Consultants Bureau

Graduate of St. Catherine's College, Cambridge University (Law). For several years a partner with Richards Butler, and now a partner at Hardwick Stallards, a City law firm with international commercial practice.

Rossiter, Ann

Director, Lexington Communications

Former Director at Fishburn Hedges, joined Lexington as Director in September 2001.

Rowe, Sam

Managing Director, GPC Brussels

Has worked with Charles Barker, McCann and Euro RSCG. More recently a Director of Hill and Knowlton's Burssels office. Joined GPC in 2001.

Royal, Phil

Senior Consultant, Butler Kelly

Worked for the Labour Party in Millbank during the 1997 General Election Campaign, with special responsibility for briefing candiates.

Ruano, George Ellis

Director, Gellis Communications

Director at Hill and Knowlton for seven years before starting Gellis communications in 1997, a Brussels-based consultancy affiliated to August.One. Considerable experience in media and communications in the context of lobbying or public policy strategy.

Sacker, Jon

Senior Consultant, GCI Political Counsel

Head of Office for Paul Tyler MP, and worked in the Liberal Democrat Policy Unit with joint responsibility for drafting the 1992 party manifesto. Also worked as Local Campaigns Officer for the Royal National Institute for the Blind. Spent three-and-a-half years as Director of Public Affairs at the Board of Deputies of British Jews.

Saren, Jane

Managing Director, GPC Scotland

Sargood, Richard

Director, Flagship Group

Graduated from London University. Heads the marketing communications team at Flagship.

Sawer, Martin

Director, APCO UK

Worked for nearly three years at 10 Downing Street in the private office of Margaret Thatcher before leaving the civil service to join APCO UK where he now heads APCO's competition practice.

Scanlan, Rory

Director, The Policy Partnership

Lived and worked in Washington DC before moving to London, at the National Democratic Institute of International Affairs and the Congressional Research Service. Then worked for Labour's Millbank Media Centre as a media and political intelligence officer. Seconded to the Wirral South by-election shortly before the 1997 General Election. Moved into public affairs, first with Beaumark, then Citigate. Joined The Policy Partnership in September 2000.

Sharif, Henneke

Account Manager, LLM Communications

Joined LLM Communications from Edexcel, the examinations body, where she was a Public Affairs Manager.

Sharkey, Andrew

Partner, Luther Pendragon

Eighteen year career in financial and corporate communicaitons, beginning with Communications Strategy before moving to Lowe Bell Financial in 1986. Joined the financial public relations division of Hill Murray where he was appointed a director. Founding director of the Ludgate Group, which he left in 1998 to join Luther Pendragon.

Sharma, Sunil

Chief Operating Officer & Finance Director

Graduate of University of New South Wales (Commerce, majoring in accountancy). In 1988, joined PR Group, Shandwick, becoming Company Accounts Manager of one of its main UK subsidiaries in 1989. Joined Ludgate in 1993, and was appointed Finance Director and Company Secretary of Ludgate Communications in 1996. Joined Cicero Consulting in 2000.

Sherbourne, Stephen

Non-Executive Director, Chime Communications

Formerly Chairman of Bell Pottinger Public Affairs, and joined the Board of Bell Pottinger's parent company, Chime Communications, as Non-Executive Director.

Silvester, Fred

Strategic Consultant, AS Biss

A Conservative MP for 17 years with 30 years experience in advertising and public affairs. During his time as MP, he was a Conservative Whip, a PPS to two Secretaries of State, a member of the Executive of the 1922 Committee and for 4 years a member of the Public Accounts Committee. He founded Advocacy in 1986, which was aquired by AS Biss in 2000.

Simpson, Hugh

Account Manager, LLM Communications

Worked in the Liberal Democrat Whips Office, and during the 1997 General Election advised the Liberal Democrat Chief Whip, Archy Kirkwood. Joined LLM Communications having previously spent a year acting as Parliamentary and General Election Adviser to the Democratic Party in South Africa.

Smith, Andrew

Managing Director, The Policy Partnership

Began his career with the Ministry of Agriculture, Fisheries and Food. Joined Ian Greer Associates, where he worked for 14 years. He was Group Managing Director when he resigned to join The Policy Partnership in 1996. He has been a candidate at a number of local government elections in London, chairman of a constituency association and the Conservative Parliamentary Candidate for the Cynon Valley at the 1992 and 1997 General Elections.

Smith, Dan

Associate Director, PPS Group

Election agent to a candidate in the Scottish Parliamentary elections and a speechwriter and adviser to Michael McMahon MSP, who represents Hamilton North and Bellshill. Spent 15 years with CWS Limited/Scottish Co-op in the Property and Development Departments culminating in his appointment as Regional Retail Propery Manager for Scotland and Northern Ireland.

Smith, Douglas

Chairman, Political Intelligence

Graduate of King's College London (History and Politics) and the LSE. After University, joined the *Daily Mirror*. Moving into public relations, became London publicity officer for the Conservative Party and then a press officer on Ted Heath's team when, as Lord Privy Seal, he was seeking Britain's entry into the European Community. After a two-year period as Head of PR for part of the British Insurance Association, he was appointed Secretary of an all-party campaign to work under Prince Philip's Patronage, to mark the 20th Anniversary of the UN. Then director of Intercapita Public Relations before moving to Planned Public Relations as Associate Director (1968-71), at that time the largest consultancy in Europe. In 1972, left PPR to found one of Britain's earliest specialist government affairs consultancies, which has since developed into the Parliamentary Monitoring Services Group, of which he is Chairman. Been both Chairman of the PRCA (1984-85), and then President of the IPR (1990). In 1990 he received the PR Week Award for Lifetime Achievement and in 1991 the Tallents Medal of the IPR. He was the first Briton to become President of the European Association of Public Relations Consultants (1992-94). In addition to his lobbying career, he has been a Conservative Councillor, holding the following positions: Hornsey Borough Council (Chairman, Housing Committee 1963-65); Haringey Council 1964-86; deputy leader, Conservative Group 1966-1970, deputy mayor 1968-69, Chairman, Planning and Development Committee 1968-70, Chairman, Personnel Committee 1969-71, Leader, Conservative Opposition 1980-84. Member of the MCC, the Foreign Press Association, and a life member of Kent Country Cricket Club.

Smith, Stuart

Director of Corporate and Public Affairs, Edelman London

Doctoral research degree from Oxford. First position in communications was with Burson Marsteller in London. Appointed Corporate Marketing and Public Affairs Manager for 3M in the UK and Ireland, advising at Board level. Then joined The Audit Commission as Head of Communications. Member of the examining panel for the UK Communications, Advertising and Marketing (CAM) Diploma. In 1992 he was invited to become a member of the Institute of Director's working party on legislative affairs.

Soames, Evie

Director, Weber Shandwick | GJW

Graduate of Trinity College, Dublin (History and Political Science). Joined Charles Barker as a political consultant in 1971. Became Managing Director of the Public Affairs Division in 1978. Director of the Franco-British Parliamentary Relations Committee, from 1991-95 she was a Council Member of the Hansard Society and from 1993-98, a director of Liberty Plc.

Soultmann, Diana

Chief Executive Officer, Flagship Group

Graduate of Keele University, Post-graduate of the LSE (Industrial Relations). Director at Good Relations, under the leadership of Anthony Good, now Chairman of the Flagship Group. Joined The Communication Group as a founding director. Left to join Royle Communications as Managing Director and formed Millbank PR as a result of an MBO. In 1999 she became CEO of Flagship.

Spencer, Tom

Executive Director, European Centre for Public Affairs

Founder member of the European Parliament and Chairman of the Foreign Affairs Committee.

Stanley, Simon

Consultant, Probus BNW

Graduate of Durham University (History), the City University (Law). Joined McKenna & Co, a City law firm, before being called to the Bar at Lincoln's Inn. Ran the Parliamentary office of Paul Boeteng MP until 1997, also working as a Legal Policy Assistant. Council member of the Royal Borough of Kensington & Chelsea and an advisory board member of the Migrant & Refugee Community Forum.

Stapely, Sue

Quiller Consultants

Graduate of Cambridge University (English), Kingston University (Law) and the College of Law. A founder member of the SDP, she was elected to its National Executive, stood as a parliamentary candidate and was also the first Chair of the 300 Group - the all-party campaign to get more women into political and public life.Before joining Quiller, she was General Counsel and a Director of the UK's leading corporate communications and design consultancy. That followed five years as Head of Public Relations for the Law Society with responsibility for public relations, public affairs and consumer campaigns. Her book Media Relations for Lawyers was published in 1995. On the Boards of the Countryside Agency, the London Academy of Music and Dramatic Art and the Spare Tyre Theatre Company. Member of the Royal Court Theatre's Development Council, and an adviser to the BBC ActionLine and Professional Marketing.

Steinberg, Bene't

Executive Vice-President, Chelgate

Starting his career in the House of Commons, Bene't was involved in the privatisation of VSEL, the ship building concern. Moving to Hill and Knowlton, he advised the Water Services Association on its strategy and tactics in relation to the Government during privatisation, before setting up their Environment Divison. After designing and implementing the strategy used by the Independent Television Association in relation to the Broadcasting Act, formed his own company assisting in ITV franchise bids. Joined Good Relations in Issues Management before moving to Chelgate.

Steward-Smith, Charles

Partner and Co-founder, Luther Pendragon; Managing Director, Pendragon Productions

Graduate of Durham University. Career in journalism, working on the *Northern Echo* before moving to the BBC where he worked on programmes ranging from *Today* and the *Financial World Tonight* to *The Nine O'Clock News* and *Newsnight*. In 1987, joined ITN where he became editor of the *News At Ten*. Co-founded Luther Pendragon with George Pitcher where he worked as Development Director until the establishment of the partnership structure in 1999. Executive director of Rock the Vote, the charity which aims to encourage young people to vote, and a founding trustee of both the European Children's Trust and Medical Emergency Relief International (Merlin).

St George, Charles

Group Director, PPS Group

In 1990, co-founded PPS with Stephen Byfield. Formerly a Director of all three companies and ran the special projects team in PPS Local and Regional. Served as a member of the Management Board of the Association of Professional Political Consultants (APPC) and of the Public Affairs Committee of the Public Relations Consultants Association (PRCA). Moved away from London to head the PPS office in Bristol.

Stranbrook, Lionel

Managing Director (Public Affairs), DLA Upstream

Has worked as an adviser to the European Commissioner responsible for education and social affairs, then as budgetary affairs adviser to the European Democratic Group in the European Parliament. He was spokesperson, speechwriter and political adviser to Lord Plumb of Coleshill, President of the European Parliament between 1987 and 1989. He was the European Affairs Director at Shandwick Public Affairs. He spent several years as the Deputy Director-General of the Advertising Association, he is the founder and Director of the Advertising Information Group.

Summerson, Hugo

Consultant, Butler Kelly

Former Conservative MP, served on the Commons Environment Select Committee and on the All-Party Parliamentary Group on Pensions. Former Treasurer of the British-Latin American Parliamentary Group. Treasurer of the Association of Conservative Parliamentary Candidates.

Swan, Jeremy

Non-Executive Director, Cicero Consulting

Graduate of St. Andrews University. Vice President of JP Morgan, joining from Chase Manhattan Bank. Member of Wandsworth Borough Council.

Thomas, Richard

Director of Public Policy, Clifford Chance

Graduate of Southampton University (LLB). Admitted as a soliciter to Freshfields in 1973, and worked for the Citizens Advice Bureau Legal Service until 1979. Head of Public Affairs and Legal Officer for the National

Consumer Council 1979-1986. Member of the Lord Chancellor's Civil Justice Review Advisory Committee and the OECD Consumer Policy Committee, as well as several other governmental and self-regulatory advisorty and governance bodies. Director of Consumer Affairs, Office of Fair Trading, 1986-1992. Joined Clifford Chance as Director of Public Policy in 1992. Author of 'Plain English for Lawyers'.

Thompson, Simon

European Client Specialist, August.One

Worked with Charles Barker and Harvard prior to joining August.One. Former councillor of the London Borough of Hammersmith and Fulham and a member of the Labour Party.

Thompson, Stuart

DLA Upstream

PhD in Political Science at the Unviersity of Aberdeen, where he is currently an honorary research fellow. Joined DLA Upstream from the Rowland Company. Author of 'A Dictionary of Labour Quotations' (Politicos, 1999) and 'The Social Democratic Dilemma' (Macmillan's, 2000).

Thornton, Malcolm (Sir)

Chairman, Keene Public Affairs

Started his career as a Pilot on the River Mersey and entered local politics in 1965 as a member of Wallasey CB Council. Served on all the major committees and, in 1968, became the youngest Passenger Transport Chairman in the country. Became Leader of the Wirral Met. District Council and Chairman of the Merseyside Districts' Liason Comittee. Spent three years as Parliamentary Private Secretary to Patrick Jenkin at the Departments of Industry and of the Environment. Member of Parliament from 1979-97 and was Chairman of the Education and Employment Select Committee from 1989-97. Has been a Director of Keene since 1992 and Chairman since 1997.

Titterington, Mark

Account Manager, LLM Communications

Previously worked as a Political Adviser at the United Nations Organisation (New York). Also worked for the Centre for Political and Diplomatic Studies. Joined LLM Communications in February 1998.

Travers, Tony

Director of Research of the Greater London Group at the LSE; Advisory Board member, Probus BNW

An Adviser on General Expenditure to the House of Commons Select Committee on Education and Employment, Science and the Arts since 1980 and an Adviser to the House of Lords Committee on Central-Local Relations since 1995. Appointed to the Audit Commission in 1992 and a member of the Council of the Hansard Society.

Turner, Fiona

The Public Affairs Company

Formerly worked for Conservative Central Office and Leeds Chamber of Commerce.

Vaizey, Ed

Board Director, Consolidated Communications

Graduate of Oxford University (History). Worked in the Conservative Research Department, working closely with Kenneth Clarke and other senior ministers. Qualified and practiced as a commercial barrister, before joining the Public Policy Unit as a director, and thereafter, Politics International. He formed Consolidated Communications Public Affairs in June 1998. On the Board of Management of the Association of Professional Political Consultants.

Vine, Christopher

Partner and Parliamentary Agent, Winckworth Sherwood

Graduate of London University (LLB, 1972). Articled Leicester City Council; qualified 1974 assistant solicitor Hertfordshire County Council 1975-78; senior assistant solicitor Merseyside County Council 1978-91; Department of the Environment, latterly as an Assistant Solicitor and a legal Assistant Secretary 1981-91; joined Winckworth & Pemberton 1991; partner since 1992. Specialises in the authorisation of major infrastructure projects, town and country planning and compulsory purchase, and in public law.

Voss, Peter

Consultant, Commonwealth Consultants Bureau

Graduate of Conville and Caius, Cambridge University. Expert in modelling financial securities data. Major projects include design of components of the London Stock Exchange's settlement system and the UK's national EFTPOS system.

Wade, Gerry

Director, Probus BNW

Was the first non-American to be assigned to the IBM Corporate Headquarters Governmental Programmes office in Washington DC, and later became Director of IBM's European Headquarters office in Brussels. As Manager of Public Affairs for IBM UK, developed a strategic and integrated approach to the management of all the company's interests in public policy. A former Chair of the Tory Reform Group, He stood twice for Parliament in 1974. He chaired the Corporate Responsibility Group during 1990/91, and has served on the boards of a range of community, cultural and public policy bodies. He is a member of the Editorial Advisory Panel of Community Affairs Briefing.

Walker, Mark

Public Affairs Director, The Waterfront Partnership

One of the Labour Party's youngest Parliamentary Candidates in the 1987 General Election. After working for British Rail from 1977-80, he joined the the headquarters of the National Union of Railwaymen. Between 1987-92, he was the Rail, Maritime and Transport Union's Deputy Political Officer, becoming Political Officer in 1992. He was a key adviser to the Labour Party up to and during the 1997 General Election campaign, and provided support to Labour policy makers in the formulation of their green paper on Transport. He joined The Waterfront Partnership in 1998.

Wallace, Emily,

Account Director, Connect Public Affairs

Former President of Loughborough Student's Union. Research Assistant to David Blunket MP before the 1997 General Election. Worked as Campaign Aide to Stephen Byers during the 1997 election. Joined Connect Public Affairs in June 1997.

Walsh, Garry

Head of Public Affairs, August. One Public Affairs

Serving councillor for a Central London local authority, and formerly a member of a Community Health Council and the Association of London Government Equalities Panel, Garry Walsh is currently a member of a Central London Race Equality Council. Following a number of years working for several Members of Parliament and Peers, in June 2000 he joined August.One.

Warner, Nigel

Senior Adviser, Lexington Communications

Former special adviser at the Cabinet Office. Joined Lexington Communications in 2001.

Weeks, Wilf

Chairman, Weber Shandwick | GJW

Head of the Private Office of the former Conservative Leader and Prime Minister, the Rt. Hon. Sir. Edward Heath MP, from 1976 to 1980. One of the three founding members in 1980 of GJW/BSMG. Chairman of the Friends of the Tate Gallery for ten years until 1999, and is now a member of the Council of Tate Britain. A Chairman of the Trustees of Dulwich Picture Gallery.

Welch, Jo

Director, Morgan Allen Moore (Cymru / Wales)

Worked for the Welsh Labour Party (1996-98), originally collating information and and endorsements of the Party from the Welsh business community and the World of Welsh Arts. Key Campaigns Officer in the twelve month run up to the 1997 General Election. Opened the Welsh division of Morgan Allen Moore in spring 1998, in the run up to the National Assembly Elections.

Wellington, Nick

Senior Consultant, Lexington Communications

Joined Lexington Communications in 2000 from Stephen Byers' private office at the DTI.

Whale, Simon

Managing Partner, Luther Pendragon

Appointed board director of The Russell Partnership, an independent London-based policy and public affiars consultancy in 1990. Joined Bell Pottinger Public Affairs in 1997 as a director. Moved to Luther Pendragon in 2000.

Wheeldon, David

Partner, Luther Pendragon

Began his career as policy researcher for a front bench MP, before moving to head the public affairs division at Profile Corporate Communications where he advised the Falkland Islands Government during its first oil exploration licensing round. Worked for a number of trade associations such as the National Association of Pension Funds. In 1997 became political director at Laura Sandys Associates and later at Charles Barker after a merger of the two companies. Joined Luther Pendragon following a spell in Australia where he advised the Deputy President of the Australian Democrats on political strategy.

Whitehouse, Christopher

Managing Director, Good News Communications

Academic background in Business Studies and Public Administration. Worked in the Houses of Parliament for 16 years for MPs and Peers, including considerable close contact with a number of All-Party Parliamentary Groups. Launched Good News Communications in 1996, who work for a wide range of blue-chip companies, trade associations, campaiging organisations and consumer groups.

Whittaker, Nigel

Chairman, Edelman Public Relations Worldwide, UK; Director, Public Affairs Retail Unit

Majority of career spent with European Retailers Kingfisher plc, which he co-founded in 1982. Joined the Main Board in 1983 and from 1986-89 took Chairmanship of one of Kingfisher's main businesses, B&Q plc. In 1989 became Group Corporate Affairs Director. Outside Kingfisher, served as Chairman of the UK Government's Deregulation Taskforce for Retail, Tourism & Small Business, playing a major role in freeing up Sunday shopping in England and Wales. Former Chairman of the British Retail Consortium and of the Confederation of British Industry's Distributive Trades Survey Panel. In 1995 he left Kingfisher and in 1997 he was made UK Chairman of Burson Marsteller. He joined Edelman in 1999 as UK Chairman and heads their newly launched Public Affairs Retail Unit.

Wiggs, Stephen

Partner and Parliamentary Agent, Winckworth Sherwood

Graduate of the University College of Wales, Aberystwyth. London Borough of Lewisham 1973-75; qualified 1976; partner Winckworth Sherwood since 1985. Member of the Heritage Railway Association. Specialises in legislation relating to public authorities, transport undertakings, port authorities, utilities and other statutory bodies.

Wilson, David

Senior Consultant, Lexington Communications

Former special adviser at DETR.

Wingate, Frank

Executive Vice-President, Chelgate

Graduate of Oxford University. Has worked as a journalist and teacher before becoming International Publicity

Manager for the Hong Kong Trade Development Council. In 1991 he founded and subsequently developed Wingate PR, and independent agency which merged with Chelgate's Hong Kong office in 1996. Headed Chelgate Asia from 1996 to 2000, responsible for all management and financial matters for Chegate's regional office. In 2000, moved to London to join the managment team.

Wood-Dow, Nicholas

Executive Vice-President, Chelgate

A former Managing Director of a London PR firm, and in 1992, was Parliamentary Candidate in Bolton South-East. Worked closely with the then Chairman of Burson-Marsteller, Terence Fane-Saunders, as an associate director. Terence Fane-Saunders founded Chelgate in 1988 and Nicholas Wood-Dow joined as Executive Vice-President. Deputy Chairman of the Environment Council and founder/chairman of the Tory Green Initiative. Established Chelgate Environment as a business division of the company, and advisers national and international organisations on air, water, land, pollution and planning matters.

4 MPs

Members of Parliament with connections to parliamentary consultancies recorded in the Register of Memebrs Interests:

Amess, David (Southend West)

Parliamentary adviser to the Caravan Club. (£1,001–£5,000)

Atkins, Charlotte (Staffordshire Moorlands)

Unpaid adviser on parliamentary matters to the British Flouridisation Society.

Atkinson, Peter (Hexham)

Parliamentary and public affairs consultant to Countryside Alliance. (£10,001–£15,000)

Baldry, Tony (Banbury)

Parliamentary adviser to the British Constructional Steelwork Association Limited. (£5,001–£10,000)
Parliamentary adviser to the Construction Industry Council. (£1,001–£5,000)

Beith, Alan (Berwick-upon-Tweed)

Consultant to Bourne Leisure Group Ltd.; a holiday park operator in Britain and overseas, on general and parliamentary matters. (£5,001–£10,000)

Bell, Stuart (Middlesbrough)

Adviser to Ernst and Young. Remuneration for parliamentary services as part of a wider agreement. (£10,000–£15,000)
Adviser to Rotch Property Group Ltd. for parliamentary services as part of a wider agreement. (£1,001–£5,000)

Browne, Desmond (Kilmarnock and Loudoun)

Parliamentary and Public Affairs Consultant to the William Hill Organisation from 8 March – 1 June 2001. (£10,001–£15,000). Remuneration received: £3,750.

Burnside, David (South Antrim)

David Burnside Associates Ltd,: communications consultancy including occasional parliamentary and governmental advice to clients in UK and overseas. (£60,001–£65,000)

Butterfield, John (Bournemouth West)

Parliamentary adviser to British Venture Capital Association (BVCA). (£10,001-£15,000)

Cash, William (Stone)

Legal and legislative adviser to Institute of Company Accountants.

Consultant to Radcliffe's, solicitors; providing legal, legislative, parliamentary and public affairs advice. Occasionally sponsors functions for the firm. (£5,000-£10,000)

Chidgey, David (Eastleigh)

Parliamentary adviser to the National Market Trader's Federation. (£1,001-£5,000)

Cormack, Sir Patrick (South Staffordshire)

Public affairs and parliamentary adviser to Machinery Users' Association (£5,001-£10,000)

Cox, Tom (Tooting)

Parliamentary adviser (unpaid) to Ancient Order of Foresters Friendly Society.

Cummings, John (Easington)

Parliamentary adviser to the National Association of Licensed House Managers. Honorary position, not remunerated in any form.

Parliamentary adviser to the National Association of Councillors. Honorary position, not remunerated in any form.

Davies, Quentin (Grantham and Stamford)

Parliamentary consultant to the Chartered Institute of Taxation. (£10,001-£15,000)

Evans, Nigel (Ribble Valley)

Consultant (including on parliamentary and political issues) to NewsMax.com.; a business news service. Remuneration in the form of shares in the company (£1,001-£5,000)

Flook, Adrian (Taunton)

Adviser to Financial Dynamics Ltd. since 1998 (since September 2000 a subsidiary of Cordiant PLC) a financial public relations consultancy. Role is primarily an educational one to explain to colleagues how Parliament, local government and the European Union work in practice and how they all interact (£16,000). (£15,001-£20,000)

Foster, Rt. Hon. Derek (Bishop Auckland)

Parliamentary consultant to 3M UK PLC. (£5,001-£10,000)

Greenway, John (Ryedale)

Parliamentary adviser to The Institute of Sales Promotion. (£1,001-£5,000)

Parliamentary adviser to The British Promotional Merchandising Association. (£1,001–£5,000)

Parliamentary adviser to Reed Exhibitions in respect of the Incentive World Exhibition. (£1,001–£5,000)

Hague, Rt. Hon. William (Richmond (Yorks))

Parliamentary adviser to the JCB Group. (£45,001–£50,000)

Hood, Jimmy (Clydesdale)

Parliamentary consultant to Scottish Coal. (£5,001–£10,000)

Howarth, George (Knowsley North and Sefton East)

Parliamentary adviser to the William Hill Organisation. (£15,001–£20,000)

Howarth, Gerald (Aldershot)

Parliamentary adviser to the Consumer Credit Association of the United Kingdom, which is the trade association representing the majority of businesses in the home credit industry. (£5,001–£10,000)

Iddon, Dr. Brian (Bolton South East)

Fellow of and parliamentary adviser to the Royal Society of Chemistry.

Illsley, Eric (Barnsley Central)

Parliamentary adviser to the Caravan Club. (£1,001–£5,000)

Lamb, Norman (North Norfolk)

Consultant to Steele and Co., solicitors. Occasional contributions to seminars and parliamentary briefings. (£5,001–£10,000)

Leigh, Edward (Gainsborough)

Parliamentary consultant to Pinnacle Insurance PLC. (£10,001–£15,000)

MacLean, Rt. Hon. David (Penrith and The Border)

Parliamentary adviser to the Police Superintendents' Association of England and Wales. (£10,001–£15,000) (Resigned September 2001).

Mandelson, Rt. Hon. Peter (Hartlepool)

Fees and honoraria from occasional speeches, lectures, talks and articles to organisations including Weber Shandwick Worldwide.

Mates, Michael (East Hampshire)

Parliamentary consultant to Smartlogik; a computer software company. (£1–£1,000)

Meale Alan (Mansfield)

Parliamentary spokesperson and consultant (unpaid) to the "Stand By Me Club", an organisation devoted to the soul music and to the promotion of the song "Stand By Me", especially the recorded versions made by the artists Ben E. King and/or Kenny Lynch.

O'Brian, Stephen (Eddisbury)

Parliamentary adviser to the Institute of Chartered Secretaries and Administrators, of which he is a Fellow (from April 2000). (£5,001-£10,000)

O'Neill, Martin (Ochil)

Parliamentary adviser to the Machine Tool Technologies Association. (£10,001-£15,000)

Parliamentary adviser to British Chemical Engineering Contractors Association. (£1,001-£5,000)

Page, Richard (South West Hertfordshire)

Parliamentary adviser to the Machine Tool Technologies Association. (£10,001-£15,000)

Palmer, Dr. Nick (Broxtowe)

Parliamentary adviser to Novartis Services; a life sciences company. (£1,001-£5,000) Full sum goes towards the costs of newsletters to constituents and other constituency-related costs.

Parliamentary adviser to Mr Richard Spinks, Chairman of vavo.com; a company specialising in internet services for the elderly. (£1,001-£5,000) Full sum goes towards the costs of newsletters to constituents and other constituency-related costs.

Shephard, Rt. Hon. Gillian (South West Norfolk)

Senior Political Adviser to the D Group, the Networking Division of Strategy International Limited; a consultancy. (£10,001-£15,000)

Steen, Anthony (Totnes)

Public affairs, parliamentary and legal adviser to the Board of Airlines of Great Britain. Fees for parliamentary advice, (£10,001-£15,000) as part of wider agreement, and funding of part-time research help.

Taylor, Sir Teddy (Rochford and Southend East)

Port of London Police Federation – Parliamentary adviser to a small force of about 50 police officers all working in Tilbury Dock, Essex. (£1-£1,000)

Parliamentary consultant to Law Holdings, Tannochside, Uddington; open cast coal mining. (£5,001-£10,000)

Widdecombe, Rt. Hon. Anne (Maidstone and The Weald)

Prison Fellowship Honorary Parliamentary Adviser.

Wiggin, Bill (Leominster)

Provision of advice on parliamentary affairs to Commerzbank. (£1,001-£5,000)

5 Codes of Conduct

The Association of Professional Political Consultants Code of Conduct

Members of the Association of Professional Political Consultants subscribe to a voluntary code of conduct. The APPC publishes a register of professional political consultants that is updated twice a year with copies being sent to the Parliamentary Commissioner for Standards, the Cabinet Office and other interested parties.

This Code of Conduct covers the activities of regulated political consultants in relation to all United Kingdom, English, Welsh, Scottish and Northern Ireland central and local government institutions. It is a condition of membership of the APPC that the member firm, its staff and non-executive consultants should accept and agree to abide by this Code for itself and that members will be jointly and severally liable for the actions of their staff in relation to the Code. Political consultants are required to endorse the Code and to adopt and observe the principles and duties set out in it in relation to their business dealings with clients and with institutions of government.

Professional political consultants stand upon the bridge between their client and departments and agencies of Government. If they are to retain the confidence of their clients and of the institutions of government with whom they have dealings, they must conduct, and be seen to conduct, their activities with the highest standards of integrity towards both, and in such a manner as to respect and not to impair, or to give the appearance of impairing, the integrity of his company, of his clients, or of the institutions concerned (hereinafter "institutions of government" should be taken to include "public body").

The duty of political consultants is to monitor the activities of the institutions of government and to enable their clients to present a proposal or a case in the most effective way to the relevant institution. This will involve consultants in providing factual and other information to their client, analysing both the client's proposal and case and the political and policy environment in which it is to be put forward, assisting clients in preparing and advocating their case and to direct it efficiently and appropriately. This Code applies equally to all clients, whether or not fee-paying.

1. In pursuance of the principles in this Code, political consultants are required not to act or engage in any practice or conduct in any manner detrimental to the reputation of the Association or the profession of political consultancy in general.
2. Political consultants must act with honesty towards clients and the institutions of government.
3. Political consultants must use reasonable endeavors to satisfy themselves of the truth and accuracy of all statements made or information provided to clients or by or on behalf of clients to institutions of government.
4. In making representations to the institutions of government, political consultants should be open in dis-

closing the identity of their clients and other information, subject always to the requirements of commercial confidentiality.

5. Political consultants must advise clients where their objectives may be illegal, unethical or contrary to professional practice, and to refuse to act for a client in pursuance of any such objective.

6. Political consultants should not make misleading, exaggerated or extravagant claims to clients about, or otherwise misrepresent, the nature or extent of their access to institutions of government or to persons in those institutions.

7. Save for entertainment and token business mementos, political consultants should not offer or give to a client any financial inducement to secure or retain that client's business; not to offer or give, or cause a client to offer or give, any financial or other incentive to a Member of either House of Parliament, the Scottish Parliament, Welsh Assembly or Northern Ireland Assembly or Greater London Assembly, to any aide or assistant of any such Member, to any member of the staff of either House of Parliament, the Scottish Parliament, Welsh Assembly or Northern Ireland Assembly or Greater London Assembly, or to any Minister or official in any institution of government; not to accept any financial or other incentive, from whatever source, that could be construed in any way as a bribe or solicitation of favour.

8. Political consultants should not place themselves in a position of potential conflict of interest, for example by acting for any client ("Client A") where, in the view of another client ("Client B") to do so would conflict with duties to Client B; appointing to their main or subsidiary board, or to the board of any body corporate in which they have a majority interest, or causing to be appointed to any parent or associated company board, any MP, MEP, sitting Peer or any member of the Scottish Parliament or the Welsh Assembly or the Northern Ireland Assembly or the Greater London Assembly; making any award of, or allowing the holding of equity in, any Member firm; or payment in money or in kind to any MP, MEP, sitting Peer or to any member of the Scottish Parliament or the Welsh Assembly or the Northern Ireland Assembly or the Greater London Assembly, or to connected persons or persons acting on their account directly or through third parties; failing to comply with any statute, Westminster or Scottish parliamentary or Welsh or Northern Ireland Assembly or Greater London Assembly resolution and adopted recommendation of the Committee on Standards in Public Life in relation to payments to a political party in any part of the United Kingdom.

9. Political consultants who are also local authority councillors are prohibited from working on a client assignment of which the objective is to influence a decision of the local authority on which they serve.

10. Political consultants must keep strictly separate from their duties and activities as political consultants any personal activity or involvement on behalf of a political party. Where any conflict may arise between consultants' professional duties and their personal political activity, the former must have precedence.

11. Political consultants must abide by the rules and conventions for the obtaining, distribution and release of parliamentary and governmental documents.

12. Political consultants must not hold, or permit any staff member to hold, any pass conferring entitlement to access to the Palace of Westminster, to the premises of the Scottish Parliament or the Welsh Assembly or the Northern Ireland Assembly or any department or agency of government.

13. Political consultants must conduct themselves in accordance with the rules of the Palace of Westminster, Scottish Parliament, Welsh Assembly, Northern Ireland Assembly or Greater London Assembly or any department or agency of government while within their precincts, and with the rules, conventions and pro-

cedures of all institutions of government.

14. Political consultants must always abide by the internal rules on declaration and handling of interests laid down by any public body on which they serve.

15. Political consultants must not exploit public servants or abuse the facilities or institutions of central or local government within the United Kingdom.

In all their activities and dealings, political consultants should be at all times aware of the importance of his observance of the principles and duties set out in this Code for the protection and maintenance of their own reputation, the good name and success of their company, and the standing of the profession as a whole.

Compliance with the APPC's Code of Conduct

The APPC is responsible for taking appropriate disciplinary action should its code of conduct be breached. The APPC has Complaints, Arbitration and Disciplinary Rules and Procedures, further details of which are available from the secretary.

Public Relations Consultants Association, Public Affairs Committee Code of Conduct

The PRCA was the very first of the UK's major professional bodies to introduce a comprehensive code covering the conduct of those of its members which undertake public affairs activity. In late 2000, as part of the Public Affairs Committee's continuous commitment to ensure our public affairs code of conduct reflects existing best practice, your committee consulted you on a number of changes (including ones properly to reflect the recent creation of the Greater London Authority). A further code revision has been the product of this timely consultation and follows this introduction. In order to help practitioners understand the content of the new code, a short FAQ has been prepared.

This Code of Conduct covers the activities of regulated political consultants in relation to all United Kingdom, English, Welsh, Scottish and Northern Ireland central and local government institutions. It is a condition of membership of the PRCA that the member firm, its staff and non-executive consultants should accept and agree to abide by this Code for itself and that members will be liable for the actions of their staff in relation to the Code. Political consultants are required to endorse the Code and to adopt and observe the principles and duties set out in it in relation to their business dealings with clients and with institutions of government.

Professional political consultants stand upon the bridge between their client and departments and agencies of Government. If they are to retain the confidence of their clients and of the institutions of government with whom they have dealings, they must conduct, and be seen to conduct, their activities with the highest standards of integrity towards both, and in such a manner as to respect and not to impair, or to give the appearance of impairing, the integrity of his company, of his clients, or of the institutions concerned (hereinafter "institutions of government" should be taken to include "public body").

The duty of political consultants is to monitor the activities of the institutions of government and to enable their clients to present a proposal or a case in the most effective way to the relevant institution. This will involve consultants in providing factual and other information to their client, analysing both the client's proposal and case and the political and policy environment in which it is to be put forward, assisting clients in preparing and advocating their case and to direct it efficiently and appropriately. This code applies to all clients, whether or not fee-paying.

In pursuance of the principles in this Code, political consultants are required not to act or engage in any practice or conduct in any manner detrimental to the reputation of the Association or the profession of political consultancy in general.

Political consultants must act with honesty towards clients and the institutions of government.

Political consultants must use reasonable endeavours to satisfy themselves of the truth and accuracy of all statements made or information provided to clients or by or on behalf of clients to institutions of government.

In making representations to the institutions of government, political consultants should be open in disclosing the identity of their clients, subject always to the requirements of commercial confidentiality.

Political consultants must advise clients where their objectives may be illegal, unethical or contrary to professional practice, and to refuse to act for a client in pursuance of any such objective.

Political consultants should not make misleading, exaggerated or extravagant claims to clients about, or otherwise misrepresent, the nature or extent of their access to institutions of government or to persons in those institutions.

Save for entertainment and token business mementoes, political consultants should not offer or give to a client any financial inducement to secure or retain that client's business; not to offer or give, or cause a client to offer or give, any financial or other incentive to a Member of either House of Parliament, the Scottish Parliament, Welsh Assembly or Northern Ireland Assembly or Greater London Assembly, to any aide or assistant of any such Member, to any member of the staff of either House of Parliament, the Scottish Parliament, Welsh Assembly or Northern Ireland Assembly or Greater London Assembly, or to any Minister or official in any institution of government; not to accept any financial or other incentive, from whatever source, that could be construed in any way as a bribe or solicitation of favour.

Political consultants should not place themselves in a position of potential conflict of interest, for example by:

- Acting for any client ("Client A") where, in the view of another client ("Client B") to do so would conflict with duties to Client B;
- Appointing to their main or subsidiary board, or to the board of any body corporate in which they have a majority interest, or causing to be appointed to any parent or associated company board, any MP, MEP, sitting Peer or any member of the Scottish Parliament or the Welsh Assembly or the Northern Ireland Assembly or the Greater London Assembly;
- Making any award of, or allowing the holding of equity in, any Member firm; or payment in money or in kind to any MP, MEP, sitting Peer or to any member of the Scottish Parliament or the Welsh Assembly or the Northern Ireland Assembly or the Greater London Assembly, or to connected persons or persons acting on their account directly or through third parties;
- Failing to comply with any statute, Westminster or Scottish parliamentary or Welsh or Northern Ireland Assembly or Greater London Assembly resolution and adopted recommendation of the Committee on Standards in Public Life in relation to payments to a political party in any part of the United Kingdom.

Political consultants who are also local authority councillors are prohibited from working on a client assignment of which the objective is to influence a decision of the local authority on which they serve.

Political consultants must keep strictly separate from their duties and activities as political consultants any personal activity or involvement on behalf of a political party. Where any conflict may arise between consultants' professional duties and their personal political activity, the former must have precedence.

Political consultants must abide by the rules and conventions for the obtaining, distribution and release of parliamentary and governmental documents set out by the institutions of government.

Political consultants must not hold, or permit any staff member to hold, any pass conferring entitlement to access to the Palace of Westminster, to the premises of the Scottish Parliament or the Welsh Assembly or the Northern Ireland Assembly or the Greater London Assembly or any department or agency of government.

Political consultants must conduct themselves in accordance with the rules of the Palace of Westminster, Scottish Parliament, Welsh Assembly, Northern Ireland Assembly or Greater London Assembly or any department or agency of government while within their precincts, and with the rules, conventions and procedures of all institutions of government.

Political consultants must always abide by internal rules on declaration and handling of interests laid down by any public body on which they serve.

Political consultants must not exploit public servants or abuse the facilities or institutions of central or local government within the United Kingdom.

In all their activities and dealings, political consultants should be at all times aware of the importance of their observance of the principles and duties set out in this Code for the protection and maintenance of their own reputation, the good name and success of their company, and the standing of the profession as a whole.

6 Lobbying in the 21st Century

A conference held on 1 November, 2001 in Kingsway Hall, London, hosted by DLA Upstream. Published with the kind permission of DLA Upstream.

The conference aimed to dissect Governments' relationships with business, interest groups and the people, and what impact recent technological innovations would have on these relationships. The erosion of government power by corporate clout, devolution and globalisation, means the whole nature of 'grass-roots campaigning' needs to be reassessed. The collection of opinions and arguments below go some way towards doing that.

The speakers included:

- Lord Clement-Jones: Chairman of Upstream, the communications and government relations practice of DLA. He was group company secretary and legal adviser of Kingfisher plc, and prior to that he was legal director with Grand Metropolitan and London Weekend Television.
- Dick Morris: President, Vote.com. Described by Time Magazine as the 'most influential private citizen in America'. He was President Clinton's chief strategist and advisor in the 1996 campaign.
- Jessica Elgood: Head of Political Research, MORI. She also runs a number of policy-related projects on behalf of the Government's Cabinet Office.
- Mark Hatcher: Global Head of Public Affairs, PricewaterhouseCoopers. He has also worked at the Lord Chancellor's Department as the Assistant Secretary of the Law Reform Committee.
- Nicholas Jones: Political Correspondent, BBC. He has been with the BBC for over 20 years, and has published a number of books including *Sultans of Spin*, and *The Control Freaks*.
- Professor Ed Grefe: Chief Political Consultant, LDS. Prof. Grefe is cited as 'the man who invented corporate grassroots programmes'. As Vice-President, Philip Morris-USA, he was credited with creating the public affairs function of the company.

Campaigns by New Social Movements Means the Suits Will Have to Learn from Swampy

Lord Clement-Jones and Dr Steve John, DLA Upstream

The political and economic shocks caused by the terrorist acts in New York and Washington on 11 September are still rippling around the world. These events have made it imperative to understand new types of social movements. The first term Labour Government's darkest hour came not from a well-organised Opposition or the media, but a rag-bag of irate lorry drivers.

The fuel protestors, much like the anti-globalisation movements, represent a new type of dissent. They are decentralised, operating in networks or cells, and making extensive use of information and communications technology in both their organisation and execution.

These protestors achieve an impact far beyond their size or resources, through their ability to move quickly. They are almost always unwilling to engage with the traditional institutions of our democracy; they are anti-lobbyists.

Yet the web they use has been heralded as the potential saviour of democracy. It is a genuinely participatory medium holding the promise of empowered citizens with new channels of access to politics and civil society. The possibilities for Internet voting, trialed in the Arizona Democratic Primary, and much discussed in Europe, exemplify these possibilities.

Only a few decades ago the average citizen had access neither to much information about those who took decisions in their name, nor to tools that they could use to do something about it. This is now changed. Many argue the Internet and mobile phones might give the man on the Clapham omnibus the abilities, access and influence of a professional lobbyist.

The power to engage, or to disrupt, is likely to pass into the hands of those whose aims may not be conducive to the orderly processes of electoral democracy. The information revolution, which spawned these possibilities, could be government's undoing. The potential for some form of direct democracy will begin to seem irresistible once the technology exists to make it secure.

Whatever the Government of the day, it will find it exceptionally difficult not to enlarge its focus groups to the level of the whole country.

Communications with legislators, which now are few and episodic and largely driven by lobbyists, are likely to become routine, normal, and extraordinarily extensive because the Internet will offer information, guidance and an easy way to get in touch.

Yet, such digital innovations will also be a problem if the institutions of Government and Parliament, as a consequence, cease to work properly. It is clear that the 'bandwidth' of democracy is already clogged, swamped in a tide of information.

The American Houses of Congress received nearly 100m e-mails last year, many of them from Dick Morris's web site Vote.com.

Our institutions were shaped by the developments in the nineteenth century. These institutions received in the last year of the 20th century more communication and information than in the whole of the previous century. Governments have no answers to stop protestors ignoring democratic means, and seeking to use the power of networked protest instead.

We have now a fast-changing plural information environment, in which politicians find it ever more difficult to control messages and the media. The Internet provides an opportunity for Governments to attain historically unprecedented levels of transparency and accountability, but only at the cost of losing the ability to command and control. Spin could be dead.

Intermediaries like public affairs companies, advisers, and the rest, will not disappear but they will have to change. New forms of protests will continue to appear and disappear – flash-flood protests and influencing campaigns with the potential to wash away more established lobbying. These viral or guerrilla techniques will be adopted by business: the suits will have to learn from Swampy. Signs exist already that digital campaigning tends to lend itself to those who are organised already, and who know what they are doing. Organisations need to ready themselves to fight back.

Internet + 24 News cycle = opportunities for campaigners

Nicholas Jones

Nicholas Jones has seen it all in over 20 years as BBC Labour Correspondent and currently as BBC Political Correspondent. He has seen the Labour Party transform from a party of leaders sipping pints in a pub and falling over on the beach into, in his words, the 'control obsessed machine that it is today.' He has seen type-writers left behind and the world move to satellite videophones and ever more sophisticated political campaigning techniques.

Jones is a correspondent with his finger on the pulse and a media and is a communications obsessive - if you doubt that refer to his latest book 'Campaign 2001'. That technology has made a big difference to the media he said was not in doubt. Delegates wiped their eyes as he spoke wistfully of the now deceased BBC cuttings library, usurped by the unstoppable rise of the Web: 'We used to have legions of people working and storing clippings but those days are long gone' he said. The Internet has transformed the media.

He confirmed that web search engines, on-line press search facilities and press wire services to the desktop had revolutionised how journalists do their jobs. This is a very useful pointer to those of us involved in campaigns - think about and protect your web presence. How much do you use IT? How far ahead are you thinking?

Jones confirmed that technological developments such as on-line media, e.g. BBC Online, FT.com and other Internet news services increased the pressure on journalists to deliver. He was adamant about the opportunity presented by all these developments from the perspective of lobbyists and pressure groups.

Jones also touched upon some of the staples that feature in contemporary political coverage, influenced by savvy political campaigners, which were not present 20 years ago. The pooled TV interview and the preference of the parties to deny the media 'arrival shots' of a politician at an engagement are two recent developments (the two most interesting moments of the 2001 campaign, the Prescott punch and the buttonholing of the PM by the angry wife of an NHS patient, both took place in the political danger zone - i.e. when the politician arrives unprotected at a destination in full view of the media and public).

Special advisers and lobbyists, said Jones, have exploited the fact that there are two things that drive political media coverage: exclusivity and access.

The result of this awareness, said Jones, meant that journalists had much fewer opportunities in 2001 to trip up political big beasts - but he would say that, wouldn't he!

In Jones's view, the link between media and political campaigns is unquestionable. The British media offers campaigners opportunities. It often has a faster heartbeat than anywhere else in the world and has ten national newspapers and a national broadcaster which is unique in Europe in fostering internal competition amongst its news gathering arms. Conversely , Jones remains surprised at what he calls the overall poor quality of Brussels based journalism.

Jones was complimentary about the skills of British political parties. They have developed a real expertise in being aggressive and skilled in using access to politicians to exercise control over content, exactly what a journalist hates. Whilst he is critical of them in many areas of substance, he believes Blair and Campbell to be master communicators.

Whilst many conference delegates agreed that the 24 hour media is increasingly subject to the price that political parties put on access, Jones's contribution (which was highly enjoyable) would have benefited from a more explicit acknowledgement that in this war of two agendas; the media versus that of a political / campaigning organisation. The media is culpable of skulduggery as any of the political parties!

Witness the seasoned political hacks who sitting on a hum-dinger of an exclusive until late in the afternoon before confronting the most inexperienced Departmental press officer with the story. Similarly Jones did not reflect on the unkind use of camera angles and cutaways to suit the agenda of the media. Nor did he mention that the media, whilst attempting to remain balanced is easily capable of bias - witness the recent expose of some of the unbalanced coverage of the Afghan conflict in the British media.

Jones has a lot of experience and was right when he says that the challenge for political campaigners is to understand the news agenda. His message from the other side of the media fence was clear- if you understand the pressures that journalists are under and if you can fill the gaps, your campaigns will succeed.

By 2010 the Westminster Parliament won't exist - it'll be a local government.
Dick Morris

Every medium has an essence, an intrinsic essence that it communicates regardless of the content that is being sent out over that medium. If you understand that essence, as a new medium comes on the political scene, you can exploit it to be so far ahead of your rival. Franklin Roosevelt realised that the essence of radio was intimacy. John F Kennedy realised that the essence of television was charisma and glamour.

The essence of the Internet is inter-activity. It is not about more information. 'The essence of the Internet is that it permits you to speak, that it makes a monologue into a dialogue.' It will turn what has for centuries been a monologue (pamphlets, speeches, radio and TV) into not just a dialogue, but a 'pluro-logue'. This new phenomenon will enforce a discipline on the sender of the communication of customisation and responsiveness. It will totally change the method by which we govern, by which we run for office, by which we lobby those who are in office.

This development will have a profound impact on government. Politician used to go by instinct and hunch when deciding whether voters would approve. Great politicians were astute at discerning the mood of the people. That shifted to politicians listening to what the media or pollsters were telling them. Now every time a politician votes they know the poll numbers on the issue they are voting on. Polling doesn't eliminate representative democracy, but it does influence it and changes its structure.

The Internet will take that one step further. If a politician votes against the majority of a private poll then he can survive. But as Morris argues 'if I ask you all to vote and you vote for A and I'm pushing B, politicians are going to be in deep trouble. If you take a position that is at variance with public opinion, that's alright. Sometimes it's even called courage. Usually punishable by death.'

Politicians who reject Internet polls will be attacked by interest groups. The number of issues that are subject to referendums will be the same as the number of issues currently subject to polling. Direct democracy will not take the place of representative democracy legally, any more than polling has, but it will create a new level of discipline that the public will be able to enforce on its elected officials.

Morris refuses to be drawn on whether these developments are good or bad. He just believes this process is inevitable. 'Democracy is like water, it finds its own level' he argues.   Morris says 'the impact of referenda will be as cataclysmic a change as the advent of polling was. All that will happen is the per cent sign will be taken away and it will just be a number. So they'll be a direct vote rather than a poll.'

These developments should be of particular interest to Europeans because in Morris's view Europeans are increasingly governed by an unchecked bureaucracy. The role of institutions like NATO, EEU, World Bank and the IMF only have tenuous links to democratic accountability. Morris draws a comparison: 'it would be as if in the United States we just were able to vote for Governor, not for President; or for Governors who appointed the President. That would be ridiculous.'

The reason that social issues are dominating political campaigns these days, and economic issues are fading, is because people now understand that national political leaders cannot control economic issues. However, there's a belief that a supranational bureaucracy controls economics. Morris believes the anti-globalisation networks are a protest over the repeal of democracy. 'These institutions which respond minutely to the fluctuations in the market, take no account of public opinion. I believe the people of Europe will vote with their fingers on the Internet, and there will be a direct democracy before there is a representative democracy because there really is no such thing as a representative democracy in Europe. The starvation of democracy in Europe will force the evolution of Internet voting.'

Not only will government change - but so will campaigns. TV will no longer be the operators of the political process. The change will be as real as when grassroots campaigning yielded to TV campaigning and advertising in the 1960s.

Politics will become dominated by email and not by television, nor even by websites. As e-mail acquires other components, like video, they will look like a customised political commercial. Political parties are collecting email addresses - to run millions of 'separate' campaigns customised to individual voters.

Morris says 'Parties will send out a survey to voters asking which issues are most important to them and how they feel about issues. Parties will then mix and match answers - ultimately you have a different campaign for everybody. No two campaigns will look alike any more than two phone numbers look alike.'

Campaigns will also become interactive. There will need to be a mix of automation and manpower to make that level of interactivity work. The next Presidential candidates will need to sit down for thirty hours in front of a camera to record their answers on every single subject. Campaign teams will then construct a system whereby a candidate can conduct a 'dialogue' with the voters, based on the video footage, so that when the voter asks 'what do you think about abortion?', the team can given the abortion answer. Morris believes that 'in effect it will look to the user like a candidate is talking live to voters about those issues.'

The fundamental assumptions of politics today all have to change - the means of message delivery; repetition and condensation of messages; and the concept of political communication as being unilateral. In essence there will be a very interactive community where the Internet will play the central role in politics that is currently played by the media.

Business Leaders Must Respond to Critics From the Anti-Globalisation Movement

Mark Hatcher

Mark Hatcher, Head of Public Affairs for PricewaterhouseCoopers and an expert in the development and implementation of strategic corporate communications programmes, believes that business leaders need to respond vigorously to critics from the anti-globalisation movement. Developing and industrial countries are committed to improving the welfare of their citizens through renewed economic growth fuelled by internationally-linked free trade and open markets. Businesses, therefore, have an unprecedented opportunity - and indeed an ethical commitment - to establish a new corporate agenda which emphasises the principle of 'doing well financially by behaving well socially.'

The role of government is being marginalised as the impact of international trade and free market liberalisation takes hold. And although consumers have no more faith in business over political and governmental actors, it is the corporate sector which has begun shaping the social agenda. The challenge, Hatcher argues, for business leaders is to 'ensure that the process of economic liberalisation and the associated social, technological, environmental and political changes are managed wisely, and to ensure that the benefits of liberalisation are spread more widely... to ensure that globalisation works for people and not just for profits.'

There are five strategic components for a sound corporate agenda which will strengthen business' commitment to healthier social welfare systems while pursuing market liberalisation.

First, although fairly straightforward, is often overlooked by corporate leaders; have something to say, and say it. Anti-globalisation protestors have effectively, and radically in many circumstances, claimed that the World Trade Organisation (WTO) is advancing Western economic goals at the expense of under-developed nations. Moreover, liberalisation critics argue that 'public services will be destroyed and democratic rights violated' if under-developed countries are forced to accept WTO agreements. Hatcher believes that 'the protesters fail to realise that business can bring investment, technology and skills to provide the essential services that the poorest countries desperately need. Business leaders not only need to respond to their critics but also to get on to the front foot to advocate the case for responsible globalisation with vigour, conviction and persistence.'

Second, the premise that new corporate agendas will need to be more transparent. Hatcher argues that 'a more globally inter-dependent world will demand greater transparency and disclosure' as businesses come under increased scrutiny from government authorities, NGOs, radical activist groups and their shareholders.

Third, 'enlightened businesses will need to invest in the regulatory and trading environment in which they want to do business, not just in their own interest but for the benefit of the wider community.' Hatcher argues that Western corporate regimes advocating increased trade harmonisation recognise the need to 'transfer knowledge and skills from the West to invest in training local people' even though they may be training their competitors of the future.

Fourth, 'the new corporate agenda will see businesses pushing for much better quality regulation in ways that include bypassing the state.' For example, Hatcher cites last year's UN Global Compact, which asked multinational corporate actors to adhere to nine basic human rights, labour relations and environmental principles. Because the decision to follow these principles is not enforceable by the UN or any other international police agency, 'these supranational codes, are not regulatory instruments in the strict legal sense, but they are a value base to promote institutional learning and provide an informed guide to corporate behaviour.'

Finally, the newfound responsibilities for corporate actors can appear to be overwhelming and can potentially distract business leaders from the ultimate goal of creating shareholder value. Hatcher, however, believes 'that the burden can, and in appropriate cases should, be shouldered.'

As multi-national corporate actors take the lead in shaping the corporate agenda, by emphasising the principle of 'doing well financially by behaving well socially,' they face a multitude of challenges. Shareholders, consumers, employees, national regulators, NGOs, activist and watchdog groups have competing goals, and attempting to placate all of them is impossible. Likewise, as Hatcher duly notes, while the law compels CEOs to maximise shareholder value, 'the number of variables which could influence the bottom line appears to be increasing at an exponential rate.'

Today's business leaders need to become proactive in using their stature and authority to effectively respond to globalisation critics, while at the same time creating a corporate social agenda that benefits international society.

Technology and Strong Relationships Ensure the Success of Corporate Grassroots Programmes
Ed Grefe

A successful grassroots communication effort includes a strategic communications plan with a tactical commitment to undertake an ongoing programme including the application of new technology. Grefe suggests that there are four primary aspects to grassroots campaigns: the use of Internet technology to target business and political campaigns; mobilising grassroots Internet activists; the need to quickly counteract hostile messages and political threats; and the concept of linking cyberspace technology to databases for telephony and direct mail.

Grefe believes political communication can be divided into two categories to mobilise your family (those closest to you) and your friends (those associated with your organisation). Broadcast communication includes traditional media categories such as television, radio, printed media (newspapers, billboards, posters). Narrowcast is focused - highlighting user-oriented media approaches such as direct mail, telephony and person-to-person contact.

The Internet is often used as both a broadcast and narrowcast communication device. Metaphorically, Grefe argues that broadcast communication can be seen as an air war, the wholesale delivery of messages, whereas the ground war, featuring the targeted delivery of messages, is represented by narrowcast communication. Understanding the difference between these two methods of communication is important when designing a grassroots campaign. The difference in these two communications methods goes far beyond simply classifying them into one category or another. It is important to note, according to Grefe, that broadcast and narrowcast have dramatically different effects on the target audience. First, the traditional broadcast methods will require 16 or 17 'hits' before the target audience is convinced of the argument. In contrast, narrowcast requires only 6 or 7 'hits'.

Personalised e-mails and faxes can be sent to individuals. LDS generates high touch and one-on-one interaction. Individuals can be given a scorecard showing how his or her legislator voted on a particular issue and LDS is able to show how the company lobbying would have voted had they sat in the Congress or in the State Legislature. Volunteers are also given access to on-line letters which allows hem to become linked to their particular legislative district or parliamentary constituency. The result is personalised letters that have an authentic feel.

Grassroots communications is an effective way to create and deliver a message through multiple channels to a targeted group of people. Organisations engaged in grassroots communications can strengthen support and renew relationships.

Engagement is the Key to Young Voter Activism

Argues Marco DeSena

From war to right-to-life issues, the voice of young adults is often heard loud and clear. They hold rallies in parks, stage protests at universities, and sit-ins at governmental institutions. But when it comes to voting and party politics, Generation X wants nothing to do with it.

There is clearly a problem with political parties and their failure to engage young people. Since the 1970s, political parties have appeared less attractive to young people who have preferred getting involved with pressure groups. The reasons may be varied – it may the radicalism or the idealism, the focus on a single issue rather than on a range of which they may only agree with a couple. Political parties are not attractive to young people - their members are old (in the case of the Conservative Party the average age of a member is over 65!), and the way they operate comes from a different century.

Young people have issues which they feel are important to them and the way they live their lives - you only have to look at Naomi Klein's book, No Logo, to see that this is the case. This means that the challenge to be confronted by 'conventional' politicians is 'how to engage'.

There seems to be a vicious cycle amongst young people's relationship with those in power. They feel that they are not taken seriously and are fundamentally disenfranchised by most campaigns. Politicians feel that if young people refuse to participate, then why bother trying to woo their vote? The blame cycle has to stop - young voter apathy is too important to ignore.

It is assumed that apathy consists of such thoughts as 'none of the issues affects me,' 'I don't understand it,' 'I'm too busy' or 'I don't have to worry about that now.' The reality is that most young adults are engaged if the issue is important to them.

Among those aged 18-24 there is a large mass of eligible voters with genuine concerns, thoughts and ideas. What young people lack in money and campaign contributions they make up for in eagerness, will and the strength to stand up for a cause they feel just.

A permanent exclusion from voting is dangerous for democracy. A failure to engage now may lead to permanent exclusion. Parties of the left are especially wary of the current situation as they have always relied on the votes of the young to win elections.

It will take time, and a combined effort between the media, the politicians, and the young people themselves. As Clarissa White, a contributor to a Hansard Society study on voter apathy writes 'the challenge to those who are keen to kindle political interest is to ensure that young people are made aware of the relevance of politics to their lives.'

It is the actions of politicians in power and the raising of certain issues up the agenda that will grab the attention of younger voters.

It may be that the use of new technology will enable political parties to talk directly to young people. It could help show that networks of interest exist and facilitate a dialogue which grabs the attention. The politician who breaks the current downward spiral will be heralded for long to come.

A Wave of E-enthusiasm Crashes on the Rocks of Cynicism at the Roundtable Discussion

Dr Phil Collins, Director of the Social Market Foundation; Craig Hoy, Editor of Epolitix.com; Tommy Hutchison, Director of the Industry Forum; Kate McCarthy, E-campaigns Manager for the Labour Party; Andrew McGuinness, Managing Director of TBWA; and Lord Newby, Chief of Staff to Charles Kennedy MP and Liberal Democrat Treasury spokesperson in the House of Lords.

The opening statements from the panel set the scene for a lively debate. Newby's comments contradicted totally with the earlier suggestions made by Dick Morris. Newby claimed that the nature of political campaigning in General Elections had remained virtually unchanged in the last twenty years and that 'boring old disciplines' still mattered. To Newby, the clarity of message which must be 'repeated and repeated and repeated' is key. This is not the Dick Morris approach.

Hutchison detected a shift where quiet lobbying is no longer enough to convince. If you really need to convince Government you have to win public opinion. He repeated a story from one of Gordon Brown's former aides which suggested that if you wanted to get Brown to change his mind you really had to scare him! McCarthy still believed that campaigning makes a difference. To her the Internet was just one of the tools available to political parties, but one that must be strategically integrated in an overall strategy. In particular, she felt that the Internet did make a difference in the 2001 General Election.

McGuinness noted general public apathy. There was a great need to confront the fact that if politicians were going to communicate effectively with the public then a new way of delivering the message was not the solution. Making that message more relevant, personalising it, making it more localised, would be the way forward. Craig Hoy believed that there is a solid case to be made for the Internet being an influence on the process of 2001 General Election. He was particularly enthusiastic about the way in which the Web communicates in a low cost way and requires no army of footsoldiers. Most importantly it affords politicians a mediated source of information.

The questions which followed these opening statements continued the challenging nature of the day. There was more discussion of the issue of the repeating of messages. Hutchison saw that it had been essential in the past, as in the 1997 General Election. But he agreed with Morris that with the Internet repetition turns people off instantly. Hutchinson was of the opinion that building up some form of momentum is crucial for internet campaigning so that the story is able to be built, building the amount of people that engage in it.

The discussion then broadened to include the link between those who are electronically excluded and the propensity to vote. Hoy noted that it was those aged under thirty who were most likely not to have turned out at the last election whereas they are the most electronically included. He was also keen to highlight the moves by some Labour politicians such as Graham Allen MP to use of the electronic media in the drafting of legislation and pre-legislative scrutiny.

McGuinness thought that the Internet played a vital role in facilitating communications and had, therefore, made business lobbying more efficient. He did not, however, believe that the Internet was a very good channel for people who are passive receivers of information. McCarthy suggested that any possible digital device that existed at the present time would not be around by the time of the next General Election. She also believed, contrary to McGuinness, that the Internet could be used as a way of engaging people in politics.

Interestingly, Newby noted that although business has probably got better at lobbying, he had not received a single piece of business lobbying through his parliamentary email address over the past four years.

The Roundtable ended on a note of solidarity. On the suggestion made by one member of the audience that spin was dead, Hutchison fundamentally disagreed believing that it was a natural human mechanism for people to try and convince each other. It would never go away. McGuinness agreed, as did McCarthy. McGuinness thought it would not die because people have neither the time nor inclination to go through such facts. It is crucial for politicians to learn from brands like FCUK and understand why that brand has a relationship with a group of people, to try and adapt that relationship to make it more relevant to their messages.

The Personal Touch

Jessica Elgood

The stay-at-home party won the 2001 General Election according to Jessica Elgood, Head of Political and Policy Research at MORI. Elgood commented on the historically low turnout at the last election. She also touched upon issues such as the need to make voting easier, general public apathy and the electorate being incapable of absorbing detailed political argument.

Elgood delivered a full explanation of the reasons, according to MORI polls, of the motivating tactics for voting behind the 2001 General Election. This led her to conclude that both civic duty and habit remain key motivating factors for voting. Interest in politics and elections remains firm and issues such as the delivery of public services and sound financial management remain central. These are the core issues. The 2001 Election was one in which two thirds of the electorate thought it was not interesting. Non-voters did not see how they could make a difference. Media coverage was more likely to make people stay at home rather than make them go out to vote.

Elgood's key recommendation was that there is a distinct requirement to reconnect with the floating voter. To do this, she suggested, more detailed policy information is required and it would be successful if there were more about old fashioned personal contact and less about managed politics. The personal touch shines through.

Looking ahead, she believed that the key challenge for the political parties was the ability to combine the personal touch, the old fashioned approach, with the new technological advances.

The Technology Utopia is Nonsense

Phil Collins

There is only one mechanism that is more systematically overrated as an agent of change than arts and that's technology argued Phil Collins, Director of the Social Market Foundation, during the Roundtable discussion. Every single utopian vision that has ever been written places technology at its centre and claims that all else will be absolutely different in every respect thereafter. 'If it's not true then it's not true now. The Internet is not the new television, television is the new television, the Internet will become like the radio' argued Collins. Major problems of democratic participation will not be solved by new mechanisms of dissemination.

Collins believes the second systematically overrated activity in political campaigning. It matters in specific circumstances. In the overwhelming number of political campaigns it doesn't matter at all. 'It is done in order to make the people doing it feel better' says Collins. There are hundreds of campaigns which have been supremely well fought and have resulted in catastrophic defeat and the psychological drive to participate in campaigning seems to Collins a denial of that basic fact. It is a dangerous and shallow assumption to suppose that new technology will alter the problems we have in Western democratic societies, that cultural democratic problems are now far less tractable than that.

Finally, the proliferation of information in the public realm is important because it is leading to a public debate which is less clear and less honest. Nothing in technological change will alter that.

Celebrity and Technology is the Key to Successful Campaigns

Liam Byrne

Powerful political campaigns will be formed from two things – celebrity plus technology. So claims Liam Byrne, former adviser to Peter Mandelson MP on General Election organisation. Byrne, now a director of E-Government Solutions ran Labour's first national campaign in the business community. Byrne's hands on approach to both politics and technology provided him with a unique insight into the workings of political parties and campaigning.

Celebrity is playing a larger role in the modern political system. What political wannabes need to understand is that in order to win hearts and minds they have first to win eyeballs. The way in which they gain access to the eyeballs is through the new media. The US is at the forefront of much of these new developments. The campaigns of Jesse Ventura (now Governor of Minnesota), with his use of the Worldwide Web as a means of disseminating information, and presidential primary candidates Bill Bradley and John McCain with their use of their celebrity status, pushed the boundaries forward.

These were, however, overshadowed by the campaign of presidential hopeful Al Gore. Gore's nomination campaign, culminating in New York on Super Tuesday was a fusion of old and new campaigning techniques. It combined high-tech with traditional forms of organisation. What was important was the capturing of attention in the first instance through the use of fame and celebrity.

The challenge is for political parties to adapt to these changes, become more responsive and in particular, to adapt to cultural changes. These are likely to be some of the toughest challenges that political parties have faced.

7 Useful Abbreviations

APPC – Association of Professional Political Consultants

ASPA – Association for Scottish Public Affairs

GAG – IPR's UK Government Affairs Group

IPR – Institute of Public Relations

MSF – Manufacturing, Science and Finance Union

NIGAG – Northern Ireland Government Affairs Group

PRCA – Public Relations Consultants Association